THE MODERN POETS SPEAK

A collection of over 300 contemporary poems, the majority written by living American and British poets.

Together or singularly, these poems offer fresh insights into what's happening now—through the poet's experiences, thoughts, and feelings.

D1650153

THE BEST OF MODERN POETRY
is an original POCKET BOOK edition.

The Best of Modern Poetry

(Original title: *Shake the Kaleidoscope*)

Edited by
Milton Klonsky

PUBLISHED BY POCKET BOOKS NEW YORK

THE BEST OF MODERN POETRY

POCKET BOOK edition published February, 1973
2nd printing.............................July, 1975

48361

, L

This original POCKET BOOK edition is printed from brand-new plates made from newly set, clear, easy-to-read type. POCKET BOOK editions are published by POCKET BOOKS, a division of Simon & Schuster, Inc., 630 Fifth Avenue, New York, N.Y. 10020. Trademarks registered in the United States and other countries.

ACKNOWLEDGMENTS AND COPYRIGHT NOTICES

Kingsley Amis for two poems from his book, *A Case of Samples.*
John Ashbery for rights outside the United States and Canada to his poem "Song" from *The Double Dream of Spring.*
Atheneum Publishers, Inc. for three poems from *The Hard Hours* by Anthony Hecht, copyright, ©, 1967, by Anthony E. Hecht; for "A Riddle for Ponge" from *The Night of Stones* by George MacBeth, copyright, ©, 1968, by George MacBeth; for three poems from *The Firescreen* by James Merrill, copy-

Contents

CONTENTS

CONTENTS

CONTENTS

CONTENTS

Foreword

"What happens when a new work of art is created," wrote T. S. Eliot in his once famous essay *Tradition and the Individual Talent,* published in 1917, "is something that happens simultaneously to all the works of art that preceded it." And not only to works of art in the past but to those that surround it in the still more unstable and kaleidoscopic present. "The existing order is complete," Eliot continues, "before the new work arrives; for order to persist after the supervention of novelty, the *whole* existing order must be, if ever so slightly, altered. . . ." So it seemed to him at that time, so, only "slightly altered" (or only "slightly, altered"), to us. The now venerable Tradition of the New, which began more than a century ago with the shattering, by Walt Whitman in the United States and Gerard Manley Hopkins in England, of the ten syllabic commandments of the iambic pentameter—and, ultimately, iambic syntax, iambic imagery, iambic forms, iambic feelings, iambic concepts—this Tradition, of which Eliot was an heir, has devolved into the self-obsessed experimentation and restless search today for the Philosopher's Stone of a new measure, equivalent to the iambic, that might transmute contemporary poetry.

For "unless the mind change," declared W. C. Williams, "unless/the stars are new measured, according/to their relative positions, the/line will not change, the necessity/will not matriculate . . ./the old will go on/repeating itself with recurring/deadliness. . . ." Williams in his lifelong dedication to the quest had the heroic faith of a Renaissance Magus. Yet despite the premature eurekas by his and Ezra Pound's various disciples claiming to have found

> *Quoi?—L'Eternité.*
> *C'est la mer allée*
> *Avec le soleil*

"it," the very restlessness of the search itself may in the future be regarded as the rootless "measure" of our times. The established Tradition of the New has, in fact, created a poetic orthodoxy as strict as any other. There still remain, though few among the young, many original but unconverted and unreconstructed poets who prefer the bars of regular metrics and the constraints of a rationalist syntax, refusing to be "sprung" by Hopkins or "freed" by Whitman. What that sybilline poet Laura Riding (whose work, unfortunately, is unavailable for publication here) once exalted as the "sacred poetic motive" was, she felt, in danger of being "obscured in the thickening opacity of the problem of poetry as a problem in the field of language." For though poems, as well we know, are made up of words, when words speak for themselves they seldom have much to say. Nonetheless, it has become increasingly evident that the so-called "Revolution of the Word" proclaimed by the avant-garde of the twenties has spun into a Permanent Revolution, with new styles and forms superseding the old at an accelerated rate.

In assembling this book, I have therefore tried to present, as if under one dome of consciousness, an overall view of the constantly shifting and multifaceted varieties of modern poetry, and so enable them (as Mallarmé put it) "to take light by their mutual reflections"; or just to mix the metaphor as well, in this Peaceable Kingdom the hairy "beat" and the tight-sphinctered "effete" have been made to lie down together in a more or less friendly, though still wary, adjacency, without suffering thereby any adulteration or miscegenation of values. What this requires of readers (and of poets, too) of different persuasions is not so much the willing suspension of disbelief, as in the early Romantic era, but of distaste, which is somewhat harder. Poets who must sweat to forge a living line despise the seemingly effortless exudations of others; while these others, in turn, put them down as academic wheezers without the divine afflatus, mere "pale high finishers of paltry blots." If good taste has thus been violated on either side, so much the better, since good taste secretly yearns to be violated.

Various poets with an affinity through style or temper-

ament have been grouped together. For this reason, a
strictly chronological order has not been imposed—Louis
Zukovsky and Charles Olson, for instance, have been
placed with their much younger "Black Mountain" prog-
eny, likewise Kenneth Fearing with the "Beats"; but the
process by which poetry has evolved from the end of World
War I up to the present can still be traced. Rather than
provide a selection in depth from any one poet, in most
cases I have chosen instead a fair sample of his/her most
recent work available or emphasized a single aspect of a
many-sided career, as in the case of e. e. cummings. I have
also included both English and American poets without
regard to nationality since, as Henry James in England
once remarked in a letter to his brother William in the
United States 75 years ago, "insistence on their difference
becomes more and more idle and pedantic," and is by now
otiose and jejune. My own greater familiarity with modern
American poetry may have caused me to tilt the balance
somewhat in its favor or even, perhaps, to have omitted
out of ignorance some new English poetry that deserves
recognition.

As compensation, however, a number of extraordinary
poets, such as Samuel Beckett, John Wheelwright, Melvin
Tolson, Stevie Smith, George Oppen, Samuel Menashe,
Russell Edson and others, appear anthologized here for the
first time, though their work has long been available. And
I have also included a broad selection of Concrete poetry,
a genre hardly more than twenty years old yet already the
most truly worldwide in scope since the spellbound picture-
poems inscribed by shamans on the walls of caves 20,000
years ago.

My reasons for excluding the work of T. S. Eliot and, but
for one exemplary poem, of *il miglior fascist* Ezra Pound,
are mainly fiscal: the exorbitant critical interest exacted
and compounded by their poetry over two generations
constitutes, as Pound himself would have agreed, a kind of
literary usury. Besides taking up space that I would rather
devote to younger and less well-known poets, their work is
readily obtainable elsewhere. The ecosystem of this book
also precludes the poetry of Hart Crane, Marianne Moore,

W. B. Yeats, Allen Tate, John Crowe Ransom, Dylan Thomas and others who helped establish the modern tradition; but in their place may be found poetry by Basil Bunting, Hugh MacDiarmid, Gertrude Stein, Louis Zukovsky, F. T. Prince, James Stephens (who eludes being pegged as "modern" or otherwise, so has been left out of most anthologies), Edwin Muir and David Jones, to name only a few, as the relative status of poets in the previous generation has been "slightly altered," according to our own changing needs and predilections. The spirit still bloweth where it listeth, no matter how closely we weave our nets to catch it.

My criterion for choosing certain poems rather than others of perhaps equal merit has been a) the less publicized rather than the more, and b) the personally authentic rather than the historically significant. I have also tried to ignore the hostilities and jactitations of competing sects and schools, each claiming to be the current embodiment of the Word, and whose adherents (as Lewis Carroll once wrote of those in his own age) "oil each other's little heads/With mutual flattery's golden slime." Finally, it should be obvious that the number of poems assigned to each poet is not necessarily an indication of importance outside this anthology: in several instances I have chosen a single poem by, say, Theodore Roethke or Robert Lowell, as a touch- or else stepping-stone of literary vectors and values.

The chance requirements of the book itself frequently determined many of the selections as well as the order in which they were placed, thus exemplifying in its structure what the composer Eric Satie, referring to his own oeuvres, called "an organized accident . . . but with the strictness of a fugue"; or as the poet W. S. Merwin described it, putting some mallarméan English on his words, "like dice in command of their own combinations." *Go litel bok.* . . .

—Milton Klonsky

Table Talk

Granted, we die for good.
Life, then, is largely a thing
Of happens to like, not should.

And that, too, granted, why
Do I happen to like red bush,
Gray grass and green-gray sky?

What else remains? But red,
Gray, green, why those of all?
That is not what I said:

Not those of all. But those.
One likes what one happens to like.
One likes the way red grows.

It cannot matter at all.
Happens to like is one
Of the ways things happen to fall.

—Wallace Stevens

The Best of
Modern Poetry

BASIL BUNTING

Ode

A thrush in the syringa sings.

'Hunger ruffles my wings, fear,
lust, familiar things.

Death thrusts hard. My sons
by hawk's beak, by stones,
trusting weak wings
by cat and weasel, die.

Thunder smothers the sky.
From a shaken bush I
list familiar things,
fear, hunger, lust.'

O gay thrush!

from *The Well of Lycopolis*

cujus potu signa
virginitatis eripiuntu

I

Advis M'est Que J'oy Regretter

Slinking by the jug-and-bottle
swingdoor I fell in with
Mother Venus, ageing, bedraggled, a
half-quartern of gin under her shawl,
wishing she was a young girl again:
'It's cruel hard to be getting old so soon.
I wonder I dont kill myself and have done with it.

I had them all on a string at one time,
lawyers, doctors, business-men:
there wasnt a man alive but would have given
all he possessed
for what they wont take now free for nothing.
I turned them down,
I must have had no sense,
for the sake of a shifty young fellow:
whatever I may have done at other times
on the sly
I was in love then and no mistake;
and him always knocking me about
and only cared for my money.
However much he shook me or kicked me I
loved him just the same.
If he'd made me take in washing he'd
only have had to say: 'Give us a kiss'
and I'd have forgotten my troubles.
The selfish pig, never up to any good!
He used to cuddle me. Fat lot of good it's done me!
What did I get out of it besides a bad conscience?

But he's been dead longer than thirty years
and I'm still here, old and skinny.
When I think about the old days,
what I was like and what I'm like now,
it fair drives me crazy to
look at myself with nothing on.
What a change!
Miserable dried up skin and bone.

But none of their Bacchic impertinence,
medicinal stout nor portwine-cum-beef.
A dram of anaesthetic, brother.
I'm a British subject if I *am* a colonial,
distilled liquor's clean.
It's the times have changed. I remember during the War
kids carrying the clap to school under their pinnies,
studying Belgian atrocities in the Sunday papers
or the men pissing in the backstreets; and grown women
sweating their shifts sticky at the smell of khaki
every little while.
Love's an encumberance to them who
rinse carefully before using, better
keep yourself to yourself.
What it is to be in the movement!
'Follow the instructions on page fortyone'
unlovely labour of love,
'or work it off in a day's walk,
a cold douche and brisk rub down,
there's nothing like it.'
Aye, tether me among the maniacs,
it's nicer to rave than reason.'

Took her round to Polymnia's, Polymnia
glowering stedfastly at the lukewarm
undusted grate grim with cinders
never properly kindled, the brass head of the
tongs creaking as she twitched them:
'Time is, was, has been.'
A gassy fizzling spun from among the cinders.
The air, an emulsion of some unnameable oil,

greased our napes. We rhymed our breath
to the mumble of coke distilling.
'What have you come for? Why have you brought the
Goddess? You who
finger the goods you cannot purchase,
snuffle the skirt you dare not clutch.
There was never love between us, never less
than when you reckoned much. A tool
not worth the negligible price. A fool
not to be esteemed for barren honesty.
Leave me alone. A long time ago
there were men in the world, dances, guitars, ah!
Tell me, Love's mother, have I wrinkles? grey hair?
teats, or dugs? calves, or shanks?
Do I wear unbecoming garments?'

'Blotched belly, slack buttock and breast,
there's little to strip for now.
A few years makes a lot of difference.
Would you have known me?
Poor old fools,
gabbing about our young days,
squatted round a bit of fire
just lit and flickering out already:
and we used to be so pretty!'

from *Villon*

Remember, imbeciles and wits,
sots and ascetics, fair and foul,
young girls with little tender tits,
that DEATH is written over all.

Worn hides that scarcely clothe the soul
they are so rotten, old and thin,
or firm and soft and warm and full—
fellmonger Death gets every skin.

All that is piteous, all that's fair,
all that is fat and scant of breath,
Elisha's baldness, Helen's hair,
is Death's collateral:

Three score and ten years after sight
of this pay me your pulse and breath
value received. And who dare cite,
as we forgive our debtors, Death?

Abelard and Eloise,
Henry the Fowler, Charlemagne,
Genée, Lopokova, all these
die, die in pain.

And General Grant and General Lee,
Patti and Florence Nightingale,
like Tyro and Antiope
drift among ghosts in Hell,

know nothing, are nothing, save a fume
driving across a mind
preoccupied with this: our doom
is, to be sifted by the wind,

heaped up, smoothed down like silly sands.
We are less permanent than thought.
The Emperor with the Golden Hands

is still a word, a tint, a tone,
insubstantial-glorious,
when we ourselves are dead and gone
and the green grass growing over us.

The Orotava Road

Four white heifers with sprawling hooves
        trundle the waggon.
    Its ill-roped crates heavy with fruit sway.
The chisel point of the goad, blue and white,
        glitters ahead,
    a flame to follow lance-high in a man's hand
who does not shave. His linen trousers
        like him want washing.
    You can see his baked skin through his shirt.
He has no shoes and his hat has a hole in it.
        'Hu! vaca! Hu! vaca!'
    he says staccato without raising his voice;
'Adios caballero' legato but
        in the same tone.
    Camelmen high on muzzled mounts
boots rattling against the panels
        of an empty
    packsaddle do not answer strangers.
Each with his train of seven or eight tied
        head to tail they
    pass silent but for the heavy bells
and plip of slobber dripping from
        muzzle to dust;
    save that on sand their soles squeak slightly.
Milkmaids, friendly girls between
        fourteen and twenty
    or younger, bolt upright on small
trotting donkeys that bray (they arch their
        tails a few inches
    from the root, stretch neck and jaw forward
to make the windpipe a trumpet)
        chatter. Jolted
    cans clatter. The girls' smiles repeat
the black silk curve of the wimple
        under the chin.
    Their hats are absurd dolls' hats
or flat-crowned to take a load.

All have fine eyes.
You can guess their balanced nakedness
under the cotton gown and thin shift.
They sing and laugh.
They say 'Adios!' shyly but look back
more than once, knowing our thoughts
and sharing our
desires and lack of faith in desire.

from *Briggflatts*

Riding silk, adrift on noon,
a spider gleams like a berry
less black than cannibal slug
but no less pat under elders
where shadows themselves are a web.
So is summer held to its contract
and the year solvent; but men
driven by storm fret,
reminded of sweltering Crete
and Pasiphae's pungent sweat,
who heard the god-bull's feet
scattering sand,
breathed byre stink, yet stood
with expectant hand
to guide his seed to its soil;
nor did flesh flinch
distended by the brute
nor loaded spirit sink
till it had gloried in unlike creation.

• • •

Furthest, fairest things, stars, free of our humbug,
each his own, the longer known the more alone,
wrapt in emphatic fire roaring out to a black flue.
Each spark trills on a tone beyond chronological compass,
yet in a sextant's bubble present and firm

places a surveyor's stone or steadies a tiller.
Then is Now. The star you steer by is gone,
its tremulous thread spun in the hurricane
spider floss on my cheek; light from the zenith
spun when the slowworm lay in her lap
fifty years ago.

The sheets are gathered and bound,
the volume indexed and shelved,
dust on its marbled leaves.
Lofty, an empty combe,
silent but for bees.
Finger tips touched and were still
fifty years ago.
Sirius is too young to remember.

Sirius glows in the wind. Sparks on ripples
mark his line, lures for spent fish.

Fifty years a letter unanswered;
a visit postponed for fifty years.

She has been with me fifty years.

Starlight quivers. I had day enough.
For love uninterrupted night.

WILLIAM CARLOS WILLIAMS

Who Is Younger Than I?

Who is younger than I?
     The contemptible twig?
that I was? stale in mind
     whom the dirt

recently gave up? Weak
     to the wind.
Gracile? Taking up no place,
too narrow to be engraved
     with the maps

of a world it never knew,
     the green and
dovegrey countries of
     the mind.

A mere stick that has
     twenty leaves
against my convolutions.
     What shall it become,

Snot nose, that I have
     not been?
I enclose it and
     persist, go on.

Let it rot, at my center.
     Whose center?
I stand and surpass
     youth's leanness.

My surface is myself.
    Under which
to witness, youth is
    buried. Roots?

Everybody has roots.

To Elsie

The pure products of America
go crazy—
mountain folk from Kentucky

or the ribbed north end of
Jersey
with its isolate lakes and

valleys, its deaf-mutes, thieves
old names
and promiscuity between

devil-may-care men who have taken
to railroading
out of sheer lust of adventure—

and young slatterns, bathed
in filth
from Monday to Saturday

to be tricked out that night
with gauds
from imaginations which have no

peasant traditions to give them
character
but flutter and flaunt

sheer rags—succumbing without
emotion
save numbed terror

under some hedge of choke-cherry
or viburnum—
which they cannot express—

Unless it be that marriage
perhaps
with a dash of Indian blood

will throw up a girl so desolate
so hemmed round
with disease or murder

that she'll be rescued by an
agent—
reared by the state and

sent out at fifteen to work in
some hard-pressed
house in the suburbs—

some doctor's family, some Elsie—
voluptuous water
expressing with broken

brain the truth about us—
her great
ungainly hips and flopping breasts

addressed to cheap
jewelry
and rich young men with fine eyes

as if the earth under our feet
were
an excrement of some sky

and we degraded prisoners
destined
to hunger until we eat filth

while the imagination strains
after deer
going by fields of goldenrod in

the stifling heat of September
Somehow
it seems to destroy us

It is only in isolate flecks that
something
is given off

No one
to witness
and adjust, no one to drive the car

The Descent

The descent beckons
    as the ascent beckoned.
        Memory is a kind
of accomplishment,
    a sort of renewal
        even
an initiation, since the spaces it opens are new places
    inhabited by hordes
        heretofore unrealized,
of new kinds—
    since their movements
        are toward new objectives
(even though formerly they were abandoned).

No defeat is made up entirely of defeat—since
the world it opens is always a place

formerly
    unsuspected. A
world lost,
    a world unsuspected,
        beckons to new places
and no whiteness (lost) is so white as the memory
of whiteness

With evening, love wakens
    though its shadows
        which are alive by reason
of the sun shining—
    grow sleepy now and drop away
        from desire
Love without shadows stirs now
    beginning to awaken
        as night
advances.

The descent
    made up of despairs
        and without accomplishment
realizes a new awakening:
        which is a reversal
of despair.
    For what we cannot accomplish, what
is denied to love,
    what we have lost in the anticipation—
        a descent follows,
endless and indestructible

~~~~~~~~~~~~~~~~~~~~~~~~~~~~~~~~

e. e. cummings

~~~~~~~~~~~~~~~~~~~~~~

ygUDuh

      ydoan
      yunnuhstan

      ydoan o
      yunnuhstan dem
      yguduh ged

      yunnuhstan dem doidee
      yguduh ged riduh
      ydoan o nudn

LISN bud LISN

         dem
         gud
         am

         lidl yelluh bas
         tuds weer goin

duhSIVILEYEzum

*

red-rag and pink-flag
blackshirt and brown

strut-mince and stink-brag
have all come to town

some like it shot
and some like it hung
and some like it in the twot
nine months young

*

oil tel duh woil doi sez
dooyuh unnurs tanmih eesez pullih nizmus tash,oi
dough un giv uh shid oi sez.   Tom
oidoughwuntuh doot,butoiguttuh
braikyooz,datswut eesez tuhmih.   (Nowoi askyuh
woodundat maik yurarstoin
green? Oilsaisough.)—Hool
spairruh luckih? Thangzkeed.   Mairsee.
Muh jax awl gawn.   Fur Croi saik
ainnoughbudih gutnutntuhplai?

                                    HAI
yoozwidduhpoimnuntwaiv un duhyookuhsumpnruddur
givusuhtoonunduhphugnting

*

remarked Robinson Jefferson

to Injustice Taughed
your story is so interested

but you make me laft
welates Wouldwoe Washington
to Lydia E. McKinley

when Buch tooked out his C.O.D.
Abe tucks it up back inley
clamored Clever Rusefelt
to Theodore Odysseus Graren't

we couldn't free the negro
because he ant
but Coolitch wiped his valley forge

with Sitting Bull's T.P.
and the duckbilled platitude lays & lays

and Lays aytash unee

                    *

Jimmie's got a goil
                    goil
                         goil,
                              Jimmie
's got a goil and
she coitnly can shimmie

when you see her shake
                         shake
                              shake,
                                   when
you see her shake a
shimmie how you wish that you was Jimmie.

Oh for such a gurl
                    gurl
                         gurl,
                              oh
for such a gurl to
be a fellow's twistandtwirl

talk about your Sal-
                    Sal-
                         Sal-,
                              talk
about your Salo
-mes but gimmie Jimmie's gal.

                    *

sh estiffl
ystrut sal
lif san
dbut sth

epoutin(gWh.ono:w
s li psh ergo
wnd ow n,
                    r
Eve .

aling 2 a
-sprout eyelands)sin
uously&them&twi
tching,begins

unununun?
butbutbut??
tonton???
ing????

—Out-&
            steps;which
flipchucking
.grins
gRiNdS

d is app ea r in gly
eyes grip live loop croon mime
nakedly hurl asquirm the
dip&giveswoop&swoon&ingly

seethe firm swirl hips whirling climb to
GIVE
(yoursmine mineyours yoursmine
!
i( )t)

*

un
der fog
's
touch

slo

ings
fin
gering
s

wli

whichs
turn
in
to whos

est

people
be
come
un

GERTRUDE STEIN

Susie Asado

Sweet sweet sweet sweet sweet tea.
    Susie Asado.
Sweet sweet sweet sweet sweet tea.
    Susie Asado.
Susie Asado which is a told tray sure.
A lean on the shoe this means slips slips hers.
When the ancient light grey is clean it is yellow, it is a
silver seller.
This is a please this is a please there are the saids to jelly.
These are the wets these say the sets to leave a crown to Incy.
Incy is short for incubus.
A pot. A pot is a beginning of a rare bit of trees. Trees
tremble, the old vats are in bobbles, bobbles which shade and
shove and render clean, render clean must.
    Drink pups.
Drink pups drink pups lease a sash hold, see it shine and
a bobolink has pins. It shows a nail.
What is a nail. A nail is unison.
Sweet sweet sweet sweet sweet tea.

The Psychology of Nations
OR
What Are You Looking At

We make a little dance.
Willie Jewetts dance in the tenth century chateau.
Soultz Alsace dance on the Boulevard Raspail
Spanish French dance on the rue de la Boetie

Russian Flemish dance on the docks.
Bread eating is a game understand me.
We laugh to please. Japanese.
And then to seize. Blocks.
Can you remember what you said yesterday.

And now we come to a picture.

A little boy was playing marbles with soldiers, he was rolling the balls and knocking down the soldiers.
Then came a presidential election.
What did he do. He met boys of every nationality and they played together
Did they like it.
In the middle of the presidential election they had a bonfire.
A policeman stopped them.
What can a policeman do, they said.
What is older than that.
Any baby can look at a list.
This is the way they won Texas.
Let us go to the right.
It is wonderful how boys can fill.
Water.
Water swells.
We swell water.
To be lapped and bloated.
With urgency and not necessity and not idiocy.
All men are intelligent.
Please beg a boy.
Then they all danced.
How can a little Pole be a baby rusher.

PART II

Readings in missions.
Who can neglect papers.
When boys make a bonfire they do not burn daily papers.
It was pleasing to have some mutton.
Suppose a presidential election comes every fourth year.

Startling, start, startles jump again.
Jump for a feather.
A feather burns.
Indians burn have burned burns.
A boy grows dark.
He can really read better better than another.
I cannot decline a celebration.
Do you remember the Fourth of July.
And do you.
Read readily and so tell them what I say.
Jump to the word of command.
Jump where
In there
Not eating beans or butter.
Not eating hair.
Not eating a little.
When the presidential election is earnest we are only a year.
A year is so far in May.
Can you love any September.
The little boy was tall.
Dear me.
I have asked a lady to burn wood.
The boy touches the wall.
The boy is tall.
I am thinking that the way to have an election is this.
You meet in the street. You meet. You have the election.
That is why horses are of no use.
We do resist horses when we are not afraid of them.
Can one expect to be a victory.
Three long thousands.
Expect to be met.
The boy is satisfied to be steady.
Study me.
Why can't we have a presidential election.

LAST PART

The boy grows up and has a presidential election.
The president is elected.
Why do the words presidential election remind you of
anything.
They remind us that the boy who was in the street is not
necessarily a poor boy.
Nor was he a poor boy then.

EPILOGUE

Veils and veils and lying down.
Lying down in shoes.
Shoes when they are new have black on the bottom.
We saw today what we will never see again a bride's
veil and a nun's veil.
Who can expect an election.
A boy who is the son of another has a memory of per-
mission.
By permission we mean print.
By print. Solution.

Settle on another in your seats.
Kisses do not make a king.
Nor noises a mother.
Benedictions come before presidents.
Words mean more.
I speak now of a man who is not a bother.
How can he not bother.
He is elected by me.
When this you see remember me.

FINIS

Preciosilla

Please be please be get, please get wet, wet naturally, naturally in weather. Could it be fire more firier. Could it be so in ate struck. Could it be gold up, gold up stringing, in it while while which is hanging, hanging in dingling, dingling in pinning, not so. Not so dots large dressed dots, big sizes, less laced, less laced diamonds, diamonds white, diamonds bright, diamonds in the in the light, diamonds light diamonds door diamonds hanging to be four, two four, all before, this bean, lessly, all most, a best, willow, vest, a green guest, guest, go go go go go go, go. Go go. Not guessed. Go go.

Toasted susie is my ice-cream.

ERNEST HEMINGWAY

Oklahoma

All of the Indians are dead
(a good Indian is a dead Indian)
Or riding in motor cars—
(the oil lands, you know, they're all rich)
Smoke smarts my eyes,
Cottonwood twigs and buffalo dung
Smoke grey in the tepee—
(or is it my myopic trachoma)

The prairies are long,
The moon rises
Ponies
Drag at their pickets.
The grass has gone brown in the summer—
(or is it the hay crop failing)

Pull an arrow out:
If you break it
The wound closes.
Salt is good too
And wood ashes.
Pounding it throbs in the night—
(or is it the gonorrhea)

Mitraigliatrice

The mills of the gods grind slowly
But the mill
Chatters in mechanical staccato.
Ugly short infantry of the mind,
Advancing over difficult terrain.
Making this Corona
Their mitrailleuse.

The Age Demanded

The age demanded that we sing
And cut away our tongue.

The age demanded that we flow
And hammered in the bung.

The age demanded that we dance
And jammed us into iron pants.

And in the end the age was handed
The sort of shit that it demanded.

DAVID JONES

from *In Parenthesis*

You can hear the silence of it:
you can hear the rat of no-man's-land
rut-out intricacies,
weasel-out his patient workings,
scrut, scrut, sscrut,
harrow out-earthly, trowel his cunning paw;
redeem the time of our uncharity, to sap his own amphibious
paradise.

You can hear his carrying-parties rustle our corruptions
through the night-weeds—contest the choicest morsels in his
tiny conduits, bead-eyed feast on us; by a rule of his nature,
at night-feast on the broken of us.

Those broad-pinioned;
blue-burnished, or brinded-back;
whose proud eyes watched
            the broken emblems
droop and drag dust,
suffer with us this metamorphosis.

These too have shed their fine feathers; these too have
slimed their dark-bright coats; these too have condescended
to dig in.

The white-tailed eagle at the battle ebb,
                where the sea wars against the river
the speckled kite of Maldon
and the crow
have naturally selected to be un-winged;
to go on the belly, to
sap   sap   sap
with festered spines, arched under the moon; furrit with
whiskered snouts the secret parts of us.

When it's all quiet you can hear them:
scrut scrut scrut
when it's as quiet as this is.

• • •

But sweet sister death has gone debauched today and stalks
on this high ground with strumpet confidence, makes no coy
veiling of her appetite but leers from you to me with all her
parts discovered.

By one and one the line gaps, where her fancy will—how-
soever they may howl for their virginity
she holds them—who impinge less on space
sink limply to a heap
nourish a lesser category of being
like those other who fructify the land
like Tristram
Lamorak de Galis
Alisand le Orphelin
Beaumains who was youngest
or all of them in shaft-shade
at strait Thermopylae
or the sweet brothers Balin and Balan
embraced beneath their single monument.

Jonathan my lovely one
on Gelboe mountain
and the young man Absalom.
White Hart transfixed in his dark lodge.
Peredur of steel arms
and he who with intention took grass of that field to be for
him the Species of Bread.

Taillefer the maker,
and on the same day,
thirty thousand other ranks.
And in the country of Bearn—Oliver
and all the rest—so many without memento
beneath the tumuli on the high hills
and under the harvest places.
But how intolerably bright the morning is where we who are
alive and remain, walk lifted up, carried forward by an effec-
tive word.

• • •

You're clumsy in your feebleness, you implicate your tin-hat rim with the slack sling of it.

Let it lie for the dews to rust it, or ought you to decently cover the working parts.

Its dark barrel, where you leave it under the oak, reflects the solemn star that rises urgently from Cliff Trench.

It's a beautiful doll for us
it's the Last Reputable Arm.

But leave it—under the oak.
leave it for a Cook's tourist to the Devastated Areas and crawl as far as you can and wait for the bearers.

Mrs. Willy Hartington has learned to draw sheets and so has Miss Melpomené; and on the south lawns,
men walk in red white and blue
under the cedars
and by every green tree
and beside comfortable waters.
But why dont the bastards come—
Bearers!—stret-cher bear-errs!
or do they divide the spoils at the Aid-Post.

But how many men do you suppose could bear away a third of us:
drag just a little further—he yet may counter-attack.

Lie still under the oak
next to the Jerry
and Sergeant Jerry Coke.

The feet of the reserves going up tread level with your fore-head; and no word for you; they whisper one with another; pass on, inward;
these latest succours:
green Kimmerii to bear up the war.

Oeth and Annoeth's hosts they were
who in that night grew

younger men
younger striplings.

The geste says this and the man who was on the field . . . and
who wrote the book . . . the man who does not know this
has not understood anything.

from *Anathemata*

In the middle silences of this night's course the blackthorn

blows white on Orcop Hill.
They do say that on this night
                    in the warm byres
shippons, hoggots and out-barns of Britain
in the closes and the pannage-runs and on the sweet lawns of
                                                          Britain
the breathing animals-all
                    do kneel.
Some may say as on this night
                    the narrow grey-rib wolves
from the dark virgin wolds and indigenous thickets of Britain,
though very hungry and already over the fosse, kneel content on the shelving berm.

If these are but grannies' tales
                    maybe that on this night
the nine crones of Glevum in Britannia Prima, and the three
heath-hags that do and do and do
                              north of the Bodotria
in a wild beyond the Agger Antonini
and all the many sisters of Afagddu
that practise transaccidentation from Sabrina Sea
                              to Dindaethwy
in Mona Insula
                                        tell their *aves*
unreversed.

For these should know, who better?
                              (whose mates
the gossips do say
                        are of the bathosphere)
that the poor mewling babe has other theophanies:
                    not then chafed of soiled swaddlings
but with his war-soiled harness tightened on his back.

What says his *mabinogi*?
                    Son of Mair, wife of jobbing carpenter
                    in via nascitur
                    lapped in hay, *parvule*.
But what does his Boast say?
                    Alpha es et O
                                    that which
                    the whole world cannot hold.
                    Atheling to the heaven-king.
                    Shepherd of Greekland.
                    Harrower of Annwn.
                    Freer of the Waters.
                    Chief Physician and
                    dux et pontifex.

                        *

                                Who did him wash
and did his swaddlings wring?
Who did and mended for him?
Who repaired for him his tunic of one weave
now in Treventum?—so it is said.
Of whom was his mother-wit?
Who was of the gladius transfixed?
                                Whose psyche
was alone found patient of such transfixion
in all the world?

                    Wherefore we malkins three
for all our sisters
                of Anglia et Walliae and of Albany

our un-witched *aves* pay
             if only on this, HER NIGHT OF ALL.
Unto the bairn, as three clerks inclining
when they confess themselves before his Stone
at the Introit-time.

                    Kneel sisters!
                    Graymalkin! Kneel.

Kneel my sweet ape

                    whose habit is to imitate.

For in the Schools, they say:

                    if he but take the posture

the old grey ass may bray a *Gloria*.

❧§❧

HUGH MacDIARMID

Of My First Love

O my first love! You are in my life forever
Like the *Eas-Coul-aulin** in Sutherlandshire
Where the Amhainnan Loch Bhig burn
Plunges over the desolate slopes of Leitir Dubh.
Silhouetted against grim black rocks
This foaming mountain torrent
With its source in desolate tarns
Is savage in the extreme
As its waters with one wild leap
Hurl over the dizzy brink
Of the perpendicular cliff-face
In that great den of nature,
To be churned into spray
In the steaming depths below.
Near its base the fall splits up

---

* The name of a waterfall, meaning "Tresses-of-Hair" in Gaelic.

Into cascades spreading out like a fan.
A legend tells how a beautiful maiden
In desperation threw herself
Over the cataract—the waters
Immediately took on the shape
Of her waving hair,
And on moonlight nights she is still to be seen
Lying near the base of the fall,
Gazing up at the tremendous cascade
Of some six hundred feet!
O my first love! Even so you lie
Near the base of my precipitous, ever lonelier and colder life
With your fair hair still rippling out
As I remember it between my fingers
When you let me unloosen first
(Over thirty chaotic years ago!)
That golden tumult forever!

O Wha's The Bride?

O wha's the bride that cairries the bunch
O' thistles blinterin' white?
Her cuckold bridegroom little dreids
What he sall ken this nicht.

For closer than gudeman can come
And closer to'r than hersel',
Wha didna need her maidenheid
Has wrocht his purpose fell.

O wha's been here afore me, lass,
And hoo did he get in?
—*A man that deed or was I born*
This evil thing has din.

And left, as it were on a corpse,
Your maidenheid to me?

—Nae lass, gudeman, sin' Time began
'S hed ony mair to gi'e.

But I can gi'e ye kindness, lad,
And a pair o' willin' hands,
And you sall ha'e my breists like stars,
My limbs like willow wands.

And on my lips ye'll heed nae mair,
And in my hair forget,
The seed o' a' the men that in
My virgin womb ha'e met. . . .

Harry Semen

I ken these islands each inhabited
Forever by a single man
Livin' in his separate world as only
In dreams yet maist folk can.

Mine's like the moonwhite belly o' a hoo
Seen in the water as a fisher draws in his line.
I canna land it nor can it ever brak awa'.
It never moves, yet seems a' movement in the brine;
A movin' picture o' the spasm frae which I was born,
It writhes again, and back to it I'm willy-nilly torn.
A' men are similarly fixt; and the difference 'twixt
    The sae-ca'd sane and insane
Is that the latter whiles ha'e glimpses o't
    And the former nane.

Particle frae particle'll brak asunder,
Ilk ane o' them mair livid than the neist.
A separate life?—incredible war o' equal lichts,
Nane o' them wi' ocht in common in the least.
Nae threid o' a' the fabric o' my thocht
Is left alangside anither; a pack
O' leprous scuts o' weasels riddlin' a plaid

    Sic thrums could never mak'.
Hoo mony shades o' white gaed curvin' owre
To yon blae centre o' her belly's flower?
Milk-white, and dove-grey, wi' harebell veins.
Ae scar in fair hair like the sun in sunlicht lay,
And pelvic experience in a thin shadow line;
Thocht canna mairry thocht as sic saft shadows dae.
Grey ghastly commentaries on my puir life,
A' the sperm that's gane for naething rises up to damn
In sick-white onanism the single seed
Frae which in sheer irrelevance I cam.
What were the odds against me? Let me coont.
What worth am I to a' that micht ha'e been?
To a' the wasted slime I'm capable o'
Appeals this lurid emission, whirlin' lint-white and green.
Am I alane richt, solidified to life,
Disjoined frae a' this searin' like a white-het knife,
And vauntin' my alien accretions here,
Boastin' sanctions, purpose, sense the endless tide
I cam frae lacks—the tide I still sae often feed?
O bitter glitter; wet sheet and flowin' sea—and what beside?

Sae the bealin' continents lie upon the seas,
   Sprawlin' in shapeless shapes a' airts,
Like ony splash that ony man can mak'
   Frae his nose or throat or ither pairts,
Fantastic as ink through blottin'-paper rins.
But this is white, white like a flooerin' gean,
Passin' frae white to purer shades o' white,
Ivory, crystal, diamond, till nae difference is seen
Between its fairest blossoms and the stars
Or the clear sun they melt into,
And the wind mixes them amang each ither
Forever, hue upon still mair dazzlin' hue.

Sae Joseph may ha'e pondered; sae a snawstorm
Comes whirlin' in grey sheets frae the shadowy sky
And only in a sma' circle are the separate flakes seen.
White, whiter, they cross and recross as capricious they fly,
Mak' patterns on the grund and weave into wreaths,

Load the bare boughs, and find lodgements in corners frae
The scourin' wind that sends a snawstorm up frae the earth
To meet that frae the sky, till which is which nae man can say.
They melt in the waters. They fill the valleys. They scale the
    peaks.
There's a tinkle o' icicles. The topmaist summit shines oot.
Sae Joseph may ha'e pondered on the coiled fire in his seed,
The transformation in Mary, and seen Jesus tak' root.

EDWIN MUIR

Hölderlin's Journey

When Hölderlin started from Bordeaux
    He was not mad but lost in mind,
For time and space had fled away
    With her he had to find.

'The morning bells rang over France
    From tower to tower. At noon I came
Into a maze of little hills,
    Head-high and every hill the same.

'A little world of emerald hills,
    And at their heart a faint bell tolled;
Wedding or burial, who could say?
    For death, unseen, is bold.

'Too small to climb, too tall to show
    More than themselves, the hills lay round.
Nearer to her, or farther? They
    Might have stretched to the world's bound.

'A shallow candour was their all,
  And the mean riddle, How to tally
Reality with such appearance,
  When in the nearest valley

'Perhaps already she I sought,
  She, sought and seeker, had gone by,
And each of us in turn was trapped
  By simple treachery.

'The evening brought a field, a wood.
  I left behind the hills of lies,
And watched beside a mouldering gate
  A deer with its rock-crystal eyes.

'On either pillar of the gate
  A deer's head watched within the stone.
The living deer with quiet look
  Seemed to be gazing on

'Its pictured death—and suddenly
  I knew, Diotima was dead,
As if a single thought had sprung
  From the cold and the living head.

'That image held me and I saw
  All moving things so still and sad,
But till I came into the mountains
  I know I was not mad.

'What made the change? The hills and towers
  Stood otherwise than they should stand,
And without fear the lawless roads
  Ran wrong through all the land.

'Upon the swarming towns of iron
  The bells hailed down their iron peals,
Above the iron bells the swallows
  Glided on iron wheels.

'And there I watched in one confounded
  The living and the unliving head.
Why should it be? For now I know
  Diotima was dead

'Before I left the starting place;
  Empty the course, the garland gone,
And all that race as motionless
  As these two heads of stone.'

So Hölderlin mused for thirty years
  On a green hill by Tübingen,
Dragging in pain a broken mind
  And giving thanks to God and men.

WALTER DE LA MARE

Napoleon

'What is the world, O soldiers?
    It is I:
I, this incessant snow,
    This northern sky;
Soldiers, this solitude
    Through which we go
      Is I.'

JAMES STEPHENS

Psychometrist

I listened to a man and he
Had no word to say to me:
Then unto a stone I bowed,
And it spoke to me aloud.

—The force that bindeth me so long,
Once sang in the linnet's song;
Now upon the ground I lie,
While the centuries go by!

—Linnets shall for joy atone
And be fastened into stone;
While, upon the waving tree,
Stones shall sing in ecstasy!

The Snare

I hear a sudden cry of pain!
There is a rabbit in a snare:
Now I hear the cry again,
But I cannot tell from where.

But I cannot tell from where
He is calling out for aid!
Crying on the frightened air,
Making everything afraid!

Making everything afraid!
Wrinkling up his little face!
As he cries again for aid;
—And I cannot find the place!

And I cannot find the place
Where his paw is in the snare!
Little One! Oh, Little One!
I am searching everywhere!

The Wind

The wind stood up, and gave a shout;
He whistled on his fingers, and

Kicked the withered leaves about,
And thumped the branches with his hand,

And said he'd kill, and kill, and kill;
And so he will! And so he will!

The Devil's Bag

I saw the Devil walking down the lane
Behind our house.—A heavy bag
Was strapped upon his shoulders and the rain
Sizzled when it hit him.
He picked a rag
Up from the ground and put it in his sack,
And grinned, and rubbed his hands.
There was a thing
Alive inside the bag upon his back
—It must have been a soul! I saw it fling
And twist about inside, and not a hole
Or cranny for escape! Oh, it was sad!
I cried, and shouted out,—*Let out that soul!*—

But he turned round, and, sure, his face went mad,
And twisted up and down, and he said *"Hell!"*
And ran away . . . Oh, mammy! I'm not well.

Nora Criona

I have looked him round and looked him through,
Know everything that he will do

In such a case, and such a case;
And when a frown comes on his face

I dream of it, and when a smile
I trace its sources in a while.

He cannot do a thing but I
Peep to find the reason why;

For I love him, and I seek,
Every evening in the week,

To peep behind his frowning eye
With little query, little pry,

And make him, if a woman can,
Happier than any man.

—Yesterday he gripped her tight
And cut her throat. And serve her right!

A Glass of Beer

The lanky hank of a she in the inn over there
Nearly killed me for asking the loan of a glass of beer;
May the devil grip the whey-faced slut by the hair,
And beat bad manners out of her skin for a year.

That parboiled ape, with the toughest jaw you will see
On virtue's path, and a voice that would rasp the dead,
Came roaring and raging the minute she looked at me,
And threw me out of the house on the back of my head!

If I asked her master he'd give me a cask a day;
But she, with the beer at hand, not a gill would arrange!
May she marry a ghost and bear him a kitten, and may
The High King of Glory permit her to get the mange.

Egan O Rahilly

Here in a distant place I hold my tongue;
I am O Rahilly!

When I was young,
Who now am young no more,
I did not eat things picked up from the shore:
The periwinkle, and the tough dog-fish
At even-tide have got into my dish!

The great, where are they now! the great had said—
This is not seemly! Bring to him instead
That which serves his and serves our dignity—
And that was done.

I am O Rahilly!
Here in a distant place he holds his tongue,
Who once said all his say, when he was young!

SARA TEASDALE

Moon's Ending

Moon, worn thin to the width of a quill,
  In the dawn clouds flying,
How good to go, light into light, and still
  Giving light, dying.

JOHN HALL WHEELOCK

A Sun, Which Is a Star

"A sun, a shadow of a magnitude,"
So Keats has written—yet what, truly, could
Come closer to pure godhead than a sun,
Which is a star! Ours not the only one,
But ours, but nearer, so that we can say
We live by starlight the night takes away,
Leaving us many stars in place of one
Yet with less starlight than there was by day
Before that nearer, brighter, star had gone—
And if those others seem too far away,
Too high to care, remember: All we are,
All that we have, is given us by a star.

FORD MADOX FORD

L'Oubli—Temps de Sécheresse

We shall have to give up watering the land
Almost altogether.
The maize must go.
But the chilis and tomatoes may still have
A little water. The gourds must go.
We must begin to give a little to the mandarines
And the lemon-trees.

             Yes . . . and the string beans.
We will do our best to save
The chrysanthemums
Because you like them.

             Then, if only another big storm will come,
Like the one of Saturday fortnight's
We may just barely do it . . . So
We might get through to the Autumn.
At any rate we are done with the season of short nights
And water, given at dusk,
Will remain in the earth until
The torrid sun and the immense North Wind
They call the mistral
Again burns up the face of the hill.

             You will find
There will be no changes in the weather now, until
October . . . August nearly over, the season of storms is done
Altogether. There will be nothing but this hot sun
And no rain at all
Until well into the Fall.

Till then we must trust to the fruits
Though the trees are dried down to the end of the roots.

The muscats are done.
The bunch that hangs by the kitchen door
Is the last but one.
But the wine-grapes and figs and the quinces will go on
Well into September.
(If you lay down some of the grapes on paper on the garret
    floor
They will shrink and grow sweeter till honey is acid beside
    them.)

How singular, vocal and sweet those birds' voices are!
For them we may thank the drouth.
Without it they never care
To come to us from the woods of the infinitely distant South.

I wish we could have saved more of the fruits but the weather
    has tried them
Beyond endurance and there's no goodness in our land.
On this side of the hill
Even the wood has hardly enough heart to give us fuel,
Though, with vine-branches in the winter days
When the sea below us is like ruffled satin
And the mistral sings an infinite number of lays in Latin
And the sky is an infinite number of subtle greys
And you crouch beside the hearth, we shall manage to make
    up a blaze
To get up and go to bed by . . . But I like the baked, severe,
    bare
Hill with the sea below and the great storms sooner or
    later . . .

And for me
There is no satisfaction greater
Than the sight of that house-side, silver-grey
And very high
With the single, black cypress against the sky

Above the hill
And the palm-heads streaming away at the mistral's will.

Well then . . . we have outlived a winter season and a season
     of Spring
And more than one harvesting
In this land where the harvests come by twos and by threes
One on another's heels.—

Do you remember what stood where the peppers and egg-
     plants now stand?
Or the opium poppies with heads like feathery wheels?
Do you remember
When the lemons were little, the oranges smaller than peas?
We have outlived sweetcorn and haricots,
The short season of plentiful water and the rose
That covered the cistern in the day of showers.
And do you remember the thin bamboo-canes?
We have outlived innumerable flowers,
The two great hurricanes
And the unnumbered battlings back and forth
Of the mistral from the Alps in the North
And of siroccos filled with the hot breath
—'Sirocco that man unto short madness hurrieth!'—
From the sands of Africa, infinite miles to the South
And, having so, ephemeral, outlived the herbs of the hill
We may, maybe, come through the drouth
To the winter's mouth
And the season of green things
And flowing cisterns and full springs.

Hark at the voices of birds in the great catalpa's shade
Hard by the hole where the swifts once made
Their nests in the rafter, thrilling all through the night.
Singular birds with their portentous, singular flight
And human voices . . .
               They came all the way
Over the sea and the bay
From Africa.

It is only our drouth
That could have lured them away so far from the South.
                    It was perhaps they
Ulysses took for the syrens, calling 'Away!'
When he took shelter here from the thunderous main . . .

And perhaps we shall never again
Hear their incomparable, full resonance
Compact of heartless wailing and indifferent mirth
And indecipherable, hurried laughter . . .
Or not on this Earth beneath the torrid sun
For they say
It is only once in a century they come this way
In time of drouth
From their eyries far to the South
In Africa.

Or perhaps we shall hear them only after,
All harvests gathered, the time of all fruits being done,
We—oh, but not too severed by time nor walking apart!
Shall pluck and cry the one to the other, walking along the
          folds of Cap Brun:
'The herb . . . Oblivion!'
For this is a corner of France,
And this, the Kingdom of the Earth beneath the Sun
And this, the garden sealed and set apart
And that, the fountain of Jouvence . . .
And, yes, you have a heart.

JOHN BETJEMAN

On Seeing an Old Poet in the
Café Royal

I saw him in the Café Royal,
   Very old and very grand.
Modernistic shone the lamplight
   There in London's fairyland.
"Devilled chicken. Devilled whitebait.
   Devil if I understand.

Where is Oscar? Where is Bosie?
   Have I seen that man before?
And the old one in the corner,
   Is it really Wratislaw?"
Scent of Tutti-Frutti-Sen-Sen
   And cheroots upon the floor.

The Arrest of Oscar Wilde at the
Cadogan Hotel

He sipped at a weak hock and seltzer
   As he gazed at the London skies
Through the Nottingham lace of the curtains
   Or was it his bees-winged eyes?

To the right and before him Pont Street
   Did tower in her new built red,
As hard as the morning gaslight
   That shone on his unmade bed,

"I want some more hock in my seltzer,
  And Robbie, please give me your hand—
Is this the end or beginning?
  How can I understand?

"So you've brought me the latest *Yellow Book:*
  And Buchan has got in it now:
Approval of what is approved of
  Is as false as a well-kept vow.

"More hock, Robbie—where is the seltzer?
  Dear boy, pull again at the bell!
They are all little better than *cretins,*
  Though this *is* the Cadogan Hotel.

"One astrakhan coat is at Willis's—
  Another one's at the Savoy:
Do fetch my morocco portmanteau,
  And bring them on later, dear boy."

A thump, and a murmur of voices—
  ("Oh why must they make such a din?")
As the door of the bedroom swung open
  And TWO PLAIN CLOTHES POLICEMEN came in:

"Mr. Woilde, we 'ave come for tew take yew
  Where felons and criminals dwell:
We must ask yew tew leave with us quoietly
  For this *is* the Cadogan Hotel."

He rose, and he put down *The Yellow Book.*
  He staggered—and, terrible-eyed,
He brushed past the palms on the staircase
  And was helped to a hansom outside.

The Heart of Thomas Hardy

The heart of Thomas Hardy flew out of Stinsford churchyard
A little thumping fig, it rocketed over the elm trees.
Lighter than air it flew straight to where its Creator
Waited in golden nimbus, just as in eighteen sixty,
Hardman and son of Brum had depicted Him in the chancel.
Slowly out of the grass, slitting the mounds in the centre
Riving apart the roots, rose the new covered corpses
Tess and Jude and His Worship, various unmarried mothers,
Woodmen, cutters of turf, adulterers, church restorers,
Turning aside the stones thump on the upturned churchyard.
Soaring over the elm trees slower than Thomas Hardy,
Weighted down with a Conscience, now for the first time
     fleshly
Taking form as a growth hung from the feet like a sponge-bag.
There, in the heart of the nimbus, twittered the heart of Hardy
There, on the edge of the nimbus, slowly revolved the corpses
Radiating around the twittering heart of Hardy,
Slowly started to turn in the light of their own Creator
Died away in the night as frost will blacken a dahlia.

EZRA POUND

The Jewel Stairs' Grievance

The jewelled steps are already quite white with dew,
It is so late that the dew soaks my gauze stockings,
And I let down the crystal curtain
And watch the moon through the clear autumn.

By Rihaku

NOTE.—Jewel stairs, therefore a palace. Grievance, therefore there is something to complain of. Gauze stockings, therefore a court lady, not a servant who complains. Clear autumn, therefore he has no excuse on account of weather. Also she has come early, for the dew has not merely whitened the stairs, but has soaked her stockings. The poem is especially prized because she utters no direct reproach.

WILLIAM EMPSON

Note on Local Flora

There is a tree native in Turkestan,
Or further east towards the Tree of Heaven,
Whose hard cold cones, not being wards to time,
Will leave their mother only for good cause;
Will ripen only in a forest fire;
Wait, to be fathered as was Bacchus once,
Through men's long lives, that image* of time's end.
I knew the Phoenix was a vegetable.
So Semele. desired her deity
As this in Kew thirsts for the Red Dawn.

---

* *That image:* the forest fire is like the final burning of the world
[W. E.].

SAMUEL BECKETT

Cascando

1.

why not merely the despaired of
occasion of
wordshed

is it not better abort than be barren

the hours after you are gone are so leaden
they will always start dragging too soon
the grapples clawing blindly the bed of want
bringing up the bones the old loves
sockets filled once with eyes like yours
all always is it better too soon than never
the black want splashing their faces
saying again nine days never floated the loved
nor nine months
nor nine lives

2.

saying again
if you do not teach me I shall not learn
saying again there is a last
even of last times
last times of begging
last times of loving
of knowing not knowing pretending
a last even of last times of saying

if you do not love me I shall not be loved
if I do not love you I shall not love

the churn of stale words in the heart again
love love love thud of the old plunger
pestling the unalterable
whey of words

terrified again
of not loving
of loving and not you
of being loved and not by you
of knowing not knowing pretending
pretending

I and all the others that will love you
if they love you

3.

unless they love you

Enueg I

Exeo in a spasm
tired of my darling's red sputum
from the Portobello Private Nursing Home
its secret things
and toil to the crest of the surge of the steep perilous bridge
and lapse down blankly under the scream of the hoarding
round the bright stiff banner of the hoarding
into a black west
throttled with clouds.

Above the mansions the algum-trees
the mountains
my skull sullenly
clot of anger

skewered aloft strangled in the cang of the wind
bites like a dog against its chastisement.

I trundle along rapidly now on my ruined feet
flush with the livid canal;
at Parnell Bridge a dying barge
carrying a cargo of nails and timber
rocks itself softly in the foaming cloister of the lock;
on the far bank a gang of down and outs would seem to
      be mending a beam.

Then for miles only wind
and the weals creeping alongside on the water
and the world opening up to the south
across a travesty of champaign to the mountains
and the stillborn evening turning a filthy green
manuring the night fungus
and the mind annulled
wrecked in wind.

I splashed past a little wearish old man,
Democritus,
scuttling along between a crutch and a stick,
his stump caught up horribly, like a claw, under his breech,
smoking.
Then because a field on the left went up in a sudden blaze
of shouting and urgent whistling and scarlet and blue ganzies
I stopped and climbed the bank to see the game.
A child fidgeting at the gate called up:
"Would we be let in Mister?"
"Certainly" I said "you would."
But, afraid, he set off down the road.
"Well" I called after him "why wouldn't you go on in?"
"Oh" he said, knowingly,
"I was in that field before and I got put out."
So on,
derelict,
as from a bush of gorse on fire in the mountain after dark,

or, in Sumatra, the jungle hymen,
the still flagrant rafflesia.

Next:
a lamentable family of grey verminous hens,
perishing out in the sunk field,
trembling, half asleep, against the closed door of a shed,
with no means of roosting.
The great mushy toadstool,
green-black,
oozing up after me,
soaking up the tattered sky like an ink of pestilence,
in my skull the wind going fetid,
the water . . .

Next:
on the hill down from the Fox and Geese into Chapelizod
a small malevolent goat, exiled on the road,
remotely pucking the gate of his field;
the Isolde Stores a great perturbation of sweaty heroes,
in their Sunday best,
come hastening down for a pint of nepenthe or moly or half
        and half
from watching the hurlers above in Kilmainham.

Blotches of doomed yellow in the pit of the Liffey;
the fingers of the ladders hooked over the parapet,
soliciting;
a slush of vigilant gulls in the grey spew of the sewer.

Ah the banner
the banner of meat bleeding
on the silk of the seas and the arctic flowers
that do not exist.

MINA LOY

Love Songs

I

Spawn of fantasies
Sifting the appraisable
Pig Cupid   his rosy snout
Rooting erotic garbage
"Once upon a time"
Pulls a weed   white star-topped
Among wild oats sown in mucous membrane
I would   an eye in a Bengal light
Eternity in a sky-rocket
Constellations in an ocean
Whose rivers run no fresher
Than a trickle of saliva

These are suspect places

I must live in my lantern
Trimming subliminal flicker
Virginal   to the bellows
Of experience
                    Colored glass.

II

At your mercy
Our Universe
Is only
A colorless onion
You derobe

Sheath by sheath
                    Remaining
A disheartening odour
About your nervy hands

                        III

            Night
Heavy with shut-flowers' nightmares

            Noon
Curled to the solitaire
Core of the
Sun

                        IV

Evolution fall foul of
Sexual equality
Prettily miscalculate
Similitude

Unnatural selection
Breed such sons and daughters
As shall jibber at each other
Uninterpretable cryptonyms
Under the moon

Give them some way of braying brassily
For caressive calling
Or to homophonous hiccoughs
Transpose the laugh
Let them suppose that tears
Are snowdrops or molasses
Or anything
Than human insufficiencies
Begging dorsal vertebrae

Let meeting be the turning
To the antipodean

And Form   a blurr
Anything
Than seduce them
To the one
As simple satisfaction
For the other

V

Shuttle-cock and battle-door
A little pink-love
And feathers are strewn

VI

Let Joy go solace-winged
To flutter whom she may concern

VII

Once in a mezzanino
The starry ceiling
Vaulted an unimaginable family
Bird-like abortions
With human throats
And Wisdom's eyes
Who wore lamp-shade red dresses
And woolen hair
One bore a baby
In a padded porte-enfant
Tied with a sarsenet ribbon
To her goose's wings

But for the abominable shadows
I would have lived
Among their fearful furniture
To teach them to tell me their secrets
Before I guessed
—Sweeping the brood clean out

VIII

Midnight empties the street
　　　　　　To the left a boy
　One wing has been washed in the rain
　　The other will never be clean any more—
Pulling door-bells to remind
Those that are snug
　　　　　　To the right a haloed ascetic
　　　　　　Threading houses
Probes wounds for souls
　—The poor can't wash in hot water—
And I don't know which turning to take—

IX

We might have coupled
In the bed-ridden monopoly of a moment
Or broken flesh with one another
At the profane communion table
Where wine is spill't on promiscuous lips
We might have given birth to a butterfly
With the daily-news
Printed in blood on its wings

X

In some
Prenatal plagiarism
Foetal buffoons
Caught tricks

From archetypal pantomime
Stringing emotions
Looped aloft

For the blind eyes
That Nature knows us with
And the most of Nature　is green

XI

Green things grow
Salads
For the cerebral
Forager's revival . . .
And flowered flummery
Upon bossed bellies
Of mountains
Rolling in the sun

XII

Shedding our petty pruderies
From slit eyes

We sidle up
To Nature
        that irate pornographist

XIII

The wind stuffs the scum of the white street
Into my lungs and my nostrils
Exhilarated birds
Prolonging flight into the night
Never reaching

〜〜〜〜〜〜〜〜〜〜〜〜〜〜〜〜〜

WALLACE STEVENS

〜〜〜〜〜〜〜〜〜〜〜

Five Grotesque Pieces

I

ONE OF THOSE HIBISCUSES OF DAMOZELS

She was all of her airs and, for all of her airs,
She was all of her airs and ears and hairs,
Her pearly ears, her jeweler's ears
And the painted hairs that composed her hair.

In spite of her airs, that's what she was. She was all
Of her airs, as surely cologne as that she was bone
Was what she was and flesh, sure enough, but airs;
Rather rings than fingers, rather fingers than hands.

How could you ever, how could think that you saw her,
Knew her, how could you see the woman that wore the beads,
The ball-like beads, the bazzling and the bangling beads
Or hear her step in the way she walked?

This was not how she walked for she walked in a way
And the way was more than the walk and was hard to see.
You saw the eye-blue, sky-blue, eye-blue, and the powdered
　　ears
And the cheeks like flower-pots under her hair.

II

HIEROGLYPHICA

People that live in the biggest houses
Often have the worst breaths.
Hey-di-ho.

The humming-bird is the national bird
Of the humming-bird.
Hey-di-ho.

X understands Aristotle
Instinctively, not otherwise.
Hey-di-ho.

Let wise men piece the world together with wisdom
Or poets with holy magic.
Hey-di-ho.

III

COMMUNICATIONS OF MEANING

The parrot in its palmy boughs
Repeats the farmer's almanac.

A duckling of the wildest blood
Convinces Athens with its quack.

Much too much thought, too little thought,
No thought at all: a guttural growl,

A snort across the silverware,
The petals flying through the air.

IV

WHAT THEY CALL RED CHERRY PIE

Meyer is a bum. He eats his pie.
He eats red cherry pie and never says—
He makes no choice of words—

Cherries are n . . . He would never say that.
He could not. Neither of us could ever say that.
But Meyer is a bum.

He says "That's what I call red cherry pie."
And that's his way. And that's my way as well.
We two share that at least.

What is it that we share? Red cherry pie
When cherries are in season, or, at least
The way we speak of it.

Meyer has my five senses. I have his.
This matters most in things that matter least.
And that's red cherry pie.

V

OUTSIDE OF WEDLOCK

The strong music of hard times,
In a world forever without a plan
For itself as a world,
Must be played on the concertina.

The poor piano forte
Whimpers when the moon above East Hartford
Wakes us to the emotion, grand fortissimo,
Of our sense of evil,

Of our sense that time has been
Like water running in a gutter

Through an alley to nowhere,
Without beginning or the concept of an end.

The old woman that knocks at the door
Is not our grandiose destiny.
It is an old bitch, an old drunk,
That has been yelling in the dark.

Sing for her the seventy-fold Amen,
White February wind,
Through banks and banks of voices,
In the cathedral-shanty,

To the sound of the concertina,
Like the voice of all our ancestors,
The *père* Benjamin, the *mère* Blandenah,
Saying we have forgot them, they never lived.

~~~~~~~~~~~~~~~~~~~~~~~~~~~~~~~~~~~~

W. H. AUDEN

~~~~~~~~~~~~~~~~~~~~~~~~~~~~~~~~~~~~

The Geography of the House

(for Christopher Isherwood)

Seated after breakfast
In this white-tiled cabin
Arabs call *the House where*
Everybody goes,
Even melancholics
Raise a cheer to Mrs.
Nature for the primal
Pleasures She bestows.

Sex is but a dream to
Seventy-and-over,
But a joy proposed un-
   -til we start to shave:
Mouth-delight depends on
Virtue in the cook, but
This She guarantees from
Cradle unto grave.

Lifted off the potty,
Infants from their mothers
Hear their first impartial
Words of worldly praise:
Hence, to start the morning
With a satisfactory
Dump is a good omen
All our adult days.

Revelation came to
Luther in a privy
(Crosswords have been solved there)
Rodin was no fool
When he cast his Thinker,
Cogitating deeply,
Crouched in the position
Of a man at stool.

All the Arts derive from
This ur-act of making,
Private to the artist:
Makers' lives are spent
Striving in their chosen
Medium to produce a
De-narcissus-ized en-
   -during excrement.

Freud did not invent the
Constipated miser:
Banks have letter boxes
Built in their façade,

Marked *For Night Deposits,*
Stocks are firm or liquid,
Currencies of nations
Either soft or hard.

Global Mother, keep our
Bowels of compassion
Open through our lifetime,
Purge our minds as well:
Grant us a kind ending,
Not a second childhood,
Petulant, weak-sphinctered,
In a cheap hotel.

Keep us in our station:
When we get pound-noteish,
When we seem about to
Take up Higher Thought,
Send us some deflating
Image like the pained ex-
   -pression on a Major
Prophet taken short.

(Orthodoxy ought to
Bless our modern plumbing:
Swift and St. Augustine
Lived in centuries,
When a stench of sewage
Ever in the nostrils
Made a strong debating
Point for Manichees.)

Mind and Body run on
Different timetables:
Not until our morning
Visit here can we
Leave the dead concerns of
Yesterday behind us,
Face with all our courage
What is now to be.

LOUIS MacNEICE

Selva Oscura

A house can be haunted by those who were never there
If there was where they were missed. Returning to such
Is it worse if you miss the same or another or none?
The haunting anyway is too much.
You have to leave the house to clear the air.

A life can be haunted by what it never was
If that were merely glimpsed. Lost in the maze
That means yourself and never out of the wood
These days, though lost, will be all your days;
Life, if you leave it, must be left for good.

And yet for good can be also where I am,
Stumbling among dark treetrunks, should I meet
One sudden shaft of light from the hidden sky
Or, finding bluebells bathe my feet,
Know that the world, though more, is also I.

Perhaps suddenly too I strike a clearing and see
Some unknown house—or was it mine?—but now
It welcomes whom I miss in welcoming me;
The door swings open and a hand
Beckons to all the life my days allow.

THEODORE SPENCER

Eden: or One View of It

We come by a terrible gate;
We go out by a terrible gate;
The thunder blares and the lightning blares,
At the trembling gates there is lightning and thunder.
In between is there green? Lilacs?
Or oranges in between the roses?
Are there flowers there at all, or a garden?

O lost flowers, abandoned garden,
Oranges lost between the roses,
Is the green lost between the lilacs,
Between the gates of trembling thunder?
Where thunder blares and lightning blares
As we enter the terrible gate;
And go out by the terrible gate.

Epitaph

She was a high-class bitch and a dandy
Prancing man was he and a dandy
Man he was with that tall lady.

I should have known that a bitch and a dandy
Dancing man—and Oh, what a dandy!—
Would with a prance of a dapper dandy
Dance into grass; and to grass that lady.

Bitch as she was—and he was a dandy
Prancing man—it makes me angry
That those dance people should stagger and bend.
I think of that dandy and bitch and am angry
That over that bitch and over that dandy
Dancing man—and Oh, what a dandy
Man he was with that tall lady!—
Only crass grass should dance in the end.

Why Weavers Object

The shuttle went weaving efficiently on and
"Ha!" said the thread as it entered the shuttle
"Now I'm alive and important!" the shuttle
Went weaving efficiently on and the thread
Was tossed in the shuttle tossed in the shuttle
Until it was firm in the cloth and the shuttle
Went weaving efficiently on and the next
Thread that came into the shuttle said "Ha!
Now I'm alive and important!" the shuttle
Went weaving efficiently on and the
Shuttle went weaving efficiently on and
"Ha!" said the thread as it entered the shuttle.

JOHN WHEELWRIGHT

Would You Think?

Does the sound or the silence make
music? When no ripples pass
over watery trees; like painted glass
lying beneath a quiet lake;
    would you think the real forest lay
    only in the reflected
    trees, which are protected
    by non-existence from the air of day?
Our blood gives voice to earth and shell,
they speak but in refracted sounds.
The silence of the dead resounds,
but what they say we cannot tell.
    Only echoes of what they taught
    are heard by living ears.
    The tongue tells what it hears
    and drowns the silence which the dead besought.
The questioning, circumambient light
the answering, luminiferous doubt
listen, and whisper it about
until the mocking stars turn bright.
    Tardy flowers have bloomed long
    but they have long been dead.
    Now on the ice, like lead
    hailstones drop loud, with a rattlesnake's song.

Father

An East Wind asperges Boston with Lynn's sulphurous brine.
Under the bridge of turrets my father built,—from turning
       sign
of CHEVROLET, out-topping our gilt State House dome
to burning sign of CARTER'S INK—drip multitudes
of checker-board shadows. Inverted turreted reflections
sleeting over axle-grease billows, through all directions
cross-cut parliamentary gulls, who toss like gourds.

    Speak. Speak to me again, as fresh saddle leather
    (Speak; talk again) to a hunter smells of heather.
    Come home. Wire a wire of warning without words.
    Come home and talk to me again, my first friend. Father
    come home, dead man, who made your mind my home.

Bread-Word Giver

John, founder of towns,—dweller in none;
Wheelwright, schismatic,—schismatic from schismatics;
friend of great men whom these great feared greatly;
Saint, whose name and business I bear with me;
rebel New England's rebel against dominion;
who made bread-giving words for bread makers;
whose blood floods me with purgatorial fire;
I, and my unliving son, adjure you:
keep us alive with your ghostly disputation
make our renunciation of dominion
mark not the escape, but the permanent of rebellion.

Speak! immigrant ancestor in blood; brain
ancestor of all immigrants I like. Speak,
who unsealed sealed wells with a flame and sword:
   'The springs that we dug clean must be kept flowing.
   If Philistines choke wells with dirt,—open

'em up clear. And we have a flaming flare
whose light is the flare that flames up in the people.

'The way we take (who will not fire and water
taken away) is this: prepare to fight. If we
fight not for fear in the night, we shall be surprised.
Wherever we live, who want present abundance
take care to show ourselves brave. If *we* do not try
they prevail. Come out,—get ready for war;
stalwart men, out and fight. Cursed
are all who'll come not against strong wrong.
First steel your swordarm and first sword.
But the second way to go? and deed to do?

'That is this: Take hold upon our foes and kill.
We are they whose power underneath a nation
breaks it in bits as shivered by iron bars.
What iron bars are these but working wills?

Toothed as spiked threshing flails we beat
hills into chaff. Wherefore, handle our second
swords with awe. They are two-edged. They cut their
    wielders' hearts.'

Fish Food

(An Obituary to Hart Crane)

As you drank deep as Thor, did you think of milk or wine?
Did you drink blood, while you drank the salt deep?
Or see through the film of light, that sharpened your rage
    with its stare,
a shark, dolphin, turtle? Did you not see the Cat
who, when Thor lifted her, unbased the cubic ground?
You would drain fathomless flagons to be slaked with
    vacuum—
The sea's teats have suckled you, and you are sunk far
in bubble-dreams, under swaying translucent vines

of thundering interior wonder. Eagles can never now
carry parts of your body, over cupped mountains
as emblems of their anger, embers to fire self-hate
to other wonders, unfolding white flaming vistas.

Fishes now look upon you, with eyes which do not gossip.
Fishes are never shocked. Fishes will kiss you, each
fish tweak you; every kiss takes bits of you away,
till your bones alone will roll, with the Gulf Stream's swell.
So has it been already, so have the carpers and puffers
nibbled your carcass of fame, each to his liking. Now
in tides of noon, the bones of your thought-suspended
    structures
gleam as you intended. Noon pulled your eyes with small
magnetic headaches; the will seeped from your blood. Seeds
of meaning popped from the pods of thought. And you fall.
    And the unseen
churn of Time changes the pearl-hued ocean;
like a pearl-shaped drop, in a huge water-clock
falling; from *came* to *go*, from *come* to *went*. And you fell.
Waters received you. Waters of our Birth in Death dissolve
    you.
Now you have willed it, may the Great Wash take you.
As the Mother-Lover takes your woe away, and cleansing
grief and you away, you sleep, you do not snore.
Lie still. Your rage is gone on a bright flood
away; as, when a bad friend held out his hand
you said, "Do not talk any more. I know you meant no harm."
What was the soil whence your anger sprang, who are deaf
as the stones to the whispering flight of the Mississippi's rivers?
What did you see as you fell? What did you hear as you sank?
Did it make you drunken with hearing?
I will not ask any more. You saw or heard no evil.

❦

SAMUEL GREENBERG

The Glass Bubbles

The motion of gathering loops of water
Must either burst or remain in a moment.
The violet colors through the glass
Throw up little swellings that appear
And spatter as soon as another strikes
And is born; so pure are they of colored
Hues, that we feel the absent strength
Of its power. When they begin they gather
Like sand on the beach: each bubble
Contains a complete eye of water.

Conduct

By a peninsula the painter sat and
Sketched the uneven valley groves.
The apostle gave alms to the
Meek. The volcano burst
In fusive sulphur and hurled
Rocks and ore into the air—
Heaven's sudden change at
The drawing tempestuous,
Darkening shade of dense clouded hues.
The wanderer soon chose
His spot of rest; they bore the
Chosen hero upon their shoulders,
Whom they strangely admired, as
The beach-tide summer of people desired.

Enigmas

I've been ill amongst my fellow kind
And yet have borne with me joys
That few sought its indulgence, bind
As dreams that press meditation's
Wanton coys o'er desired revelation.
Religion's chariot halted for my thought;
Art bowed, showed its infinite tongues
Of charm; science hailed its width
Of symmetry, doubting conscience's
Concentration and behave; the beam
Of fire from the sun cast mine own
To slumber in imagination of spheres.
Under the heavens of moon-like shapes
Mine eyelids shut; I fell into unfelt realms.

CHARLES REZNIKOFF

Showing a torn sleeve, with stiff and shaking fingers the old
    man
pulls off a bit of the baked apple, shiny with sugar,
eating with reverence food, the great comforter.

*

These days the papers in the street
leap into the air or burst across the lawns—
not a scrap but has the breath of life:

these in a gust of wind
play about,
those for a moment lie still and sun themselves.

*

In steel clouds
to the sound of thunder
like the ancient gods:
our sky, cement;
the earth, cement;
our trees, steel;
instead of sunshine,
a light that has no twilight,
neither morning nor evening,
only noon.

Coming up the subway stairs, I thought the moon
only another street-light—
a little crooked.

*

What are you doing in our street among the automobiles,
    horse?
How are your cousins, the centaur and the unicorn?

*

If there is a scheme,
perhaps this too is in the scheme,
as when a subway car turns on a switch,
the wheels screeching against the rails,
and the lights go out—
but are on again in a moment.

*

About an excavation
a flock of bright red lanterns
has settled.

*

When the sky is blue, the water over the sandy bottom is
    green.
They have dropped newspapers on it, cans, a bedspring, sticks
    and stones;
but these the patient waters corrode, those a patient moss
    covers.

*

ASYLUM PRODUCT

Brown and black felt, unevenly stitched with purple thread;
what unhappiness is perpetuated in the brown and black of
    this pincushion,
lunatic?

*

Here, beggar, three pennies—
your fare to serenity:
abstinence, reticence, diligence—
hunger, silence, and sweat.

*

RAINY SEASON

It has been raining for three days.
The faces of the giants
on the billboards
still smile,
but the gilt has been washed from the sky:
we see the iron world.

MELVIN TOLSON

MU

Hideho Heights
and I, like the brims of old hats,
slouched at a sepulchered table in the Zulu Club.
Frog Legs Lux and his Indigo Combo
spoke with tongues that sent their devotees
out of this world!

Black and brown and yellow fingers flashed,
like mirrored sunrays of a heliograph,
on clarinet and piano keys, on cornet valves.

Effervescing like acid on limestone,
Hideho said:
"O White Folks, O Black Folks,
the dinosaur imagined its extinction meant
the death of the piss ants."

Cigarette smoke
—opaque veins in Carrara marble—
magicked the habitués into
humoresques and grotesques.
Lurid lights
spraying African figures on the walls
ecstasied maids and waiters,
pickups and stevedores—
with delusions
of Park Avenue grandeur.

Once, twice,
Hideho sneaked a swig.

"On the house," he said, proffering the bottle
as he lorded it under the table.
Glimpsing the harpy eagle at the bar,
I grimaced,
"I'm not the house snake of the Zulu Club."

A willow of a woman,
bronze as knife money,
executed, near our table, the Lenox Avenue Quake.
Hideho winked at me and poked
that which
her tight Park Avenue skirt vociferously advertised.
Peacocking herself, she turned like a ballerina,
her eyes blazing drops of rum on a crêpe suzette.
"Why, you—"
A sanitary decree, I thought. "Don't *you* me!" he fumed.
The lips of a vixen exhibited a picadill flare.
"*What* you smell isn't cooking," she said.
Hideho sniffed.
"Chanel No. 5," he scoffed,
"from Sugar Hill."
I laughed and clapped him on the shoulder.
"A bad metaphor, *poet*."
His jaws closed
like an alligator squeezer.
"She's a willow," I emphasized,
"a willow by a cesspool."
Hideho mused aloud,
'Do I hear The Curator rattle Eliotic bones?"

Out of the Indigo Combo
flowed rich and complex polyrhythms.
Like surfacing bass,
exotic swells and softenings
of the veld vibrato
emerged.
• • •

Was that Snakehips Briskie
gliding out of the aurora australis of the Zulu Club
into the kaleidoscopic circle?

. . .

Etnean gasps!
Vesuvian acclamations!

. . .

Snakehips poised himself—
Giovanni Gabrieli's
single violin against his massed horns.

. . .

The silence of the revelers was the arrested
hemorrhage of an artery
grasped by bull forceps.
I felt Hideho's breath against my ear.
"The penis act in the Garden of Eden," he confided.

. . .

Convulsively, unexampledly,
Snakehips' body and soul
began to twist and untwist like a gyrating rawhide—
began to coil, to writhe
like a prismatic-hued python
in the throes of copulation.
Eyes bright as the light
at Eddystone Rock,
an ebony Penthesilea
grabbed her tiger's-eye yellow-brown
beanpole Sir Testiculus of the evening
and gave him an Amazonian hug.
He wilted in her arms
like a limp morning-glory.
"The Zulu Club is in the groove," chanted Hideho,
"and the cats, the black cats, are *gone!*"

In the *ostinato*
of stamping feet and clapping hands,
the Promethean bard of Lenox Avenue became a
lost loose-leaf
as memory vignetted
Rabelaisian I's of the Boogie-Woogie dynasty

in barrel houses, at rent parties,
on riverboats, at wakes:
The Toothpick, Funky Five, and Tippling Tom!
Ma Rainey, Countess Willie V., and Aunt Harriet!
Speckled Red, Skinny Head Pete, and Stormy Weather!
Listen, Black Boy.
Did the High Priestess at 27 rue de Fleurus
assert, "The Negro suffers from nothingness"?
Hideho confided like a neophyte on The Walk,
"Jazz is the marijuana of the Blacks."
In the *tribulum* of dialectics, I juggled the idea;
then I observed,
"Jazz is the philosophers' egg of the Whites."

Hideho laughed from below the Daniel Boone rawhide belt
he'd redeemed, in a Dallas pawn shop,
with part of the black-market
loot set loose
in a crap game
by a Yangtze ex-coolie who,
in a Latin Quarter dive below Telegraph Hill,
out-Harvarded his Alma Mater.
• • •
Frog Legs Lux and his Indigo Combo
let go
with a wailing pedal point
that slid into
Basin Street Blues
like Ty Cobb stealing second base:
Zulu,
King of the Africans,
arrives on Mardi Gras morning;
the veld drum of Baby Dodds'
great-grandfather
in Congo Square
pancakes the first blue note
in a callithump of the USA.
And now comes the eve of Ash Wednesday.
Comus on parade!
All God's children revel

like a post-Valley Forge
charivari in Boston celebrating the nuptials of
a gay-old-dog minuteman with a lusty maid.

• • •

Just as
the bourgeois adopted
the lyric-winged piano of Liszt in the court at Weimar
for the solitude of his
aeried apartment,
Harlem chose
for its cold-water flat
the hot-blues cornet of King Oliver
in his cart
under the
El pillars of the Loop.

• • •

The yanking fishing rod
of Hideho's voice
jerked me out of my bird's-foot violet romanticism.
He mixed Shakespeare's image with his own
and caricatured me:
"Yonder Curator has a lean and hungry look;
he thinks too much.
Such blackamoors are dangerous to
the Great White World!"

• • •

With a dissonance
from the Weird Sisters,
the jazz diablerie
boiled down and away
in the vacuum pan
of the Indigo Combo.

from *Psi*

For dark hymens on the auction block,
the lord of the mansion knew the macabre score:
not a dog moved his tongue,
not a lamb lost a drop of blood to protect a door.

O
Xenos of Xanthos,
what midnight-to-dawn lecheries,
in cabin and big house,
produced these brown hybrids and yellow motleys?

White Boy,
Buchenwald is a melismatic song
whose single syllable is sung to blues notes
to dark wayfarers who listen for the gong
at the crack of doom along
. . . that Lonesome Road . . .
before they travel on.

A Pelagian with the *raison d'être* of a Negro,
I cannot say I have outwitted dread,
for I am conscious of the noiseless tread
of the Yazoo tiger's ball-like pads behind me
in the dark
as I trudge ahead,
up and up . . . that Lonesome Road . . . up and up.

In a Vision in a Dream,
from the frigid seaport of the proud Xanthochroid,
the good ship *Défineznegro*
sailed fine, under an unabridged moon,
to reach the archipelago
Nigeridentité.
In the Strait of Octoroon,
off black Scylla,
after the typhoon Phobos, out of the Stereotypus Sea,
had rived her hull and sail to a T,
the *Défineznegro* sank the rock
and disappeared in the abyss
(Vanitas vanitatum!)
of white Charybdis.

YVOR WINTERS

Song of the Trees

Belief is blind! Bees scream!
Gongs! Thronged with light!

       And I take
into light, hold light,
in light I live, I,
pooled and broken here,
to watch, to wake above you.

       Sun,
no seeming, but savage
simplicity, breaks running
for an aeon, stops, shuddering, here.

The Rows of Cold Trees

To be my own Messiah to the
burning end. Can one endure the
acrid, steeping darkness of
the brain, which glitters and is
dissipated? Night. The night is
winter and a dull man bending,
muttering above a freezing pipe;
and I, bent heavily on books; the
mountain iron in my sleep and
ringing; but the pipe has frozen, haired with
unseen veins, and cold is on the eyelids: who can
remedy this vision?

                              I have walked upon
the streets between the trees that
grew unleaved from asphalt in a night of
sweating winter in distracted silence.

                                    I have
walked among the tombs—the rushing of the air
in the rich pines above my head is that which
ceaseth not nor stirreth whence it is:
in this the sound of wind is like a flame.

It was the dumb decision of the
madness of my youth that left me with
this cold eye for the fact; that keeps me
quiet, walking toward a
stinging end: I am alone,
and, like the alligator cleaving timeless mud,
among the blessed who have Latin names.

A Dream Vision

What was all the talk about?
This was something to decide.
It was not that I had died.
Though my plans were new, no doubt,
There was nothing to deride.

I had grown away from youth,
Shedding error where I could;
I was now essential wood,
Concentrating into truth:
What I did was small but good.

Orchard tree beside the road,
Bare to core, but living still!
Moving little was my skill.
I could hear the farting toad
Shifting to observe the kill,

Spotted sparrow, spawn of dung,
Mumbling on a horse's turd,
Bullfinch, wren, or mockingbird
Screaming with a pointed tongue
Objurgation without word.

J. V. CUNNINGHAM

Haecceity

Evil is any this or this
Pursued beyond hypothesis.

It is the scribbling of affection
On the blank pages of perfection.

Evil is presentness bereaved
Of all the futures it conceived,

Wilful and realized restriction
Of the insatiate forms of fiction.

It is this poem, or this act.
It is this absolute of fact.

Epigrams

Arms and the man I sing, and sing for joy,
Who was last year all elbows and a boy.

*

Deep sowing of our shame, rage of our need,
Gross shadow of Idea, impersonal seed,
Unclothed desire! the malice of your thrust
Is his to use who takes his love on trust.

*

In this child's game where you grow warm and warmer,
And new grand passions still exceed the former,
In what orgasm of high sentiment
Will you conclude and sleep at last content?

*

Career was feminine, resourceful, clever.
You'd never guess to see her she felt ever
By a male world oppressed. How much they weigh!
Even her hand disturbed her as she lay.

*

You wonder why *Drab* sells her love for gold?
To have the means to buy it when she's old.

*

Soft found a way to damn me undefended:
I was forgiven who had not offended.

*

And now you're ready who while she was here
Hung like a flag in a calm. Friend, though you stand
Erect and eager, in your eye a tear,
I will not pity you, or lend a hand.

*

On a cold night I came through the cold rain
And false snow to the wind shrill on your pane

With no hope and no anger and no fear:
Who are you? and with whom do you sleep here?

*

I know not what I am. I think I know
Much of the circumstance in which I flow.
But knowledge is not power; I am that flow
Of history and of percept which I know.

*

Time heals not: it extends a sorrow's scope
As goldsmiths gold, which we may wear like hope.

*

Good Fortune, when I hailed her recently,
Passed by me with the intimacy of shame
As one that in the dark had handled me
And could no longer recollect my name.

*

I had gone broke, and got set to come back,
And lost, on a hot day and a fast track,
On a long shot at long odds, a black mare
By Hatred out of Envy by Despair.

*

All in due time: love will emerge from hate,
And the due deference of truth from lies.
If not quite all things come to those who wait
They will not need them: in due time one dies.

*

Grief restrains grief as dams torrential rain,
And time grows fertile with extended pain.

*

How we desire desire! Joy of surcease
In joy's fulfillment is bewildered peace,
And harsh renewal. Life in fear of death
Will trivialize the void with hurrying breath,
With harsh indrawal. Nor love nor lust impels us.
Time's hunger to be realised compels us.

*

Dark thoughts are my companions. I have wined
With lewdness and with crudeness, and I find
Love is my enemy, dispassionate hate
Is my redemption though it come too late—
Though I come to it with a broken head
In the cat-house of the dishevelled dead.

Montana Fifty Years Ago

Gaunt kept house with her child for the old man,
Met at the train, dust-driven as the sink
She came to, the child white as the alkali.
To the West distant mountains, the Big Lake
To the Northeast. Dead trees and almost dead
In the front yard, the front door locked and nailed,
A handpump in the sink. Outside, a land
Of gophers, cottontails, and rattlesnakes,
In good years of alfalfa, oats, and wheat.
Root cellar, blacksmith shop, milk house, and barn,
Granary, corral. An old *World Almanac*
To thumb at night, the child coughing, the lamp smoked,
The chores done. So he came to her one night,
To the front room, now bedroom, and moved in.
Nothing was said, nothing was ever said.
And then the child died and she disappeared.
This was Montana fifty years ago.

ELDER OLSON

Punch and Judy Songs

BUTCHER

A butcher has to handle flesh,
That cannot be denied;
Why not that dainty morsel?
That's what I thought, and died.

BAKER

That oven was hot as hot,
With nothing at all inside;
Why should he grudge my little loaf?
That's what I thought, and died.

CANDLESTICK-MAKER

Although I dealt in candlesticks,
A certain candle was my pride;
Why not that fancy socket for it?
That's what I thought, and died.

JUDY

His hate was generous as love,
I had the costliest gems to wear;
What jewel's more costly than a tear?

Passion I had abundance of,
Passion that pierced me to the marrow;
What passion runs more deep than sorrow?

PUNCH

A woman on her back is good,
Better is a woman on her knees;
Change all your sweetly simpering loves
To spitting, clawing enemies:

I slept with her three thousand nights,
Had no such pleasure from her bed,
No such shuddering ecstasy,
As on the night I choked her dead.

HANGMAN

Silence is the most delicate music,
Though difficult to hear;
None dance so delicately
As hanged men dancing upon air.

Leap and bow and swing, my pretty,
There's nothing daintier anywhere;
None dance so delicately
As hanged men dancing upon air.

Able, Baker, Charlie, et al.

The grass hissed, then
Power and phone lines broke,
Cocoanuts flew like cannonballs,
Palm trees bent double, and most snapped,
Tin roofs took off and scaled about,
Slashed legs or arms or heads from all they met.
The shacks went somersaulting this way and that, like tum-
      bleweeds,
The coffee industry blew out like a match.
One house, to show what it could do,
Got up from its foundations and waddled off,
As if sick of everything, turned back to lumber;
A second committed suicide; jumped from the cliff.

A whole wood thought it was time that the world saw its roots,
And showed them, leaping up into the air
And staying there, locked into a fantastic arch
You can still walk under. One family
Cowering in the cellar, heard a fearful crash
And learned, next day, they had an extra roof
(The one who had lost it knew about it sooner).
Another found that fish can fly in flocks,
Given reason enough. Robertson and his friends,
Groping in the dark of boarded windows,
Groped from room to room as something removed
Room after room; ended up packed tight, bolt-upright in the
tiny kitchen,
Twenty-three persons, four kids standing in the kitchen sink
Of a house that had shrunk to a kitchen.
The boats in the harbor really caught it; all but the big
freighter
Listened to their anchors.
Got convinced it was no wetter at the bottom
And a heck of a lot safer; so they went to it.

Robertson, squinting out a crack in the shutter
Through absolutely horizontal rain
At a vegetable world writhing with pain, and shrieking with
it, too,
Saw a funny thing: one old moth-eaten cow, left out in a field,
Knew she was trapped, turned her rump to the source of the
trouble,
Braced legs, and stood that way through the whole business,
Though her bags slapped the tar out of her sides, and vice
versa.
Next morning, at least she was there, and damn little else was,
The green had even been knocked out of the grass, as if
autumn had come
(A thing it never does). Robertson thought,
There's more hell than anything, what you pick up in one jam
Might work in the next; he got three things out of this one:
First, that when everything behaves unnaturally,
The cause is still natural; secondly,

The fools who go out in the lull get hit by the second
    installment;
The third he got from the cow; it has nothing to do with
    patient endurance of difficulties,
But is somewhat indecent; at least, he puts it indecently;
And it mayn't save you, but it will relieve your feelings.

F. T. PRINCE

False Bay

> She I love leaves me, and I leave my friends
> In the dusky capital where I spent two years
> In the cultivation of divinity.
> Sitting beside my window above the sea
> In this unvisited land I feel once more
> How little ingenious I am. The winter ends,
> The seaward slopes are covered to the shore
> With a press of lilies that have silver ears.
> And although I am perplexed and sad, I say
> 'Now indulge in no dateless lamentations:
> Watch only across the water the lapsed nations
> And the fisherman twitch a boat across the bay.'

Words from Edmund Burke

To the vigilance of my exertion a lax pause,
Offering in the vehicle and wavering colour of evening
My weakness to my judgement, whether it may be a fault
Of defect or excess in me, or whether most
Not from a sort of habit of having what I say go for nothing?

For although I had allowed (I hardly shall allow)
That fable of persuasion, should I have no title to surprise
Upon felicitations of failure? And yet it is the time,
And I own as I ought to do, I have failed, I shall fail
Failing with the aid of all the images you may choose
For the proprieties of sentiment and the canons
Of a liquid eloquence; of links
Of favouring lights, of medals, of hinges, my grammar
My logic, vocables like fagots, triple cords, gongs, florets
A whole chivalry of leaves: I mean
An inordinate number of decorated reflections branching
Into how many more I have hinted at, as well as joints
Fans and ligaments and horns. I am an artisan of fire.

Far as this our business bearing me, thus far am I led to set
My ripe steps on a way I see before me, a soft pace
That tests it as to the use I may be of in the sorrows we
Have seen too much of. But since the times
Will come to worse: and neither the senate nor the soldier, not
     seeing
As I do, great London like a fuscous rose, her door-ways
Warm with the flux of quality, her shops bundles of muslin
     sown with rubies,
Her frigates tilted above the mud at low tide, and the town
Like a heap of fresh wet stars; and neither
The mushrooms of her markets, nor her polity nor her pravity
Will observe the secreted city of the speaker: let then this
Be to the other a sepulchre. Advanced I have my city,
And under the glimmering decadence of heaven, deepened,
Displayed the broad and dividing streets, the close columns
Of a sea-stone, the straitened palaces, the shallow quadrants
Vacated theatres, full graves and the temple trembling
To the least word. And I have watched it,

And in vain. And in vain before it I have turned
Too completely the religious animal. My thought, sight,
And what I saw a song; my instruments must intricately
Simulate an involuntary ascension, melt in flight.
And that austere insolence of tune was (nowhere near
The loud grudge of levellers) a manner of grovelling

To some tyranny of snow at morning. And all
To be connected it may be with the fact
That I came once from abroad, bred
In a transmarine province, whence
The more my eyes, my tongue the more might
Cling to the forms I have laboured to obtain; and so,
All the constructions put upon what I would be at, in that I
    would
Drink with my own looks, touch with my own hands, were
Eminently subject, being of a soft rash love
To the defamations of boyish fates, and the rudeness of those
    who would glory
In a revolution of things. I hope I

Am as little awed out of my wits by the fear
Of vulgar shrewdness, as most of those I esteem. I have
    neglected
To follow, to bow to fortune. Yet if I love, I may lie:
And if I shine, obloquy will have it as a serpent
Who's in love with how he shines. And of a truth there is
This of wonderful in it that I should then
Prove no stronger than my passion: the machinery
Is itself well enough to answer all ends,
Were the matter but as sound; but what will serve
The arrangement of rottenness? Why should I build
With pain, were it with honour, and besieged by much foul
    gold,
On such frail stuff as the state? Why for an art
The lowest choose, choose also to revive
What other men no longer would believe? But so I must:
The fire that's born of peace returns to peace,
No phoenixhood resides in a transparence.
I should have died into the death I saw. And so I choose,

And to undertake the odious office of a priest
Among a diseased and desperate people, prosperous urchins
With the condescension of a conscious victim visit. Suffer,
Restore the flown thing. Sorrow with palms
Would 'fallen fallen light renew'. So I rejoice
To resign the lustres of a true success,

Myself to be what I pursued or praised, and so delight
To proclaim that cunning agony of rectitude, that my actions
Shifts and equivocations, all were and will be answers
To an immense mass of dark dealings. The system stretching
    now
To tracts that will be rank in future ruins, in both worlds
There is now this fistulous sore that runs
Into a thousand sinuosities; and the wound now
Opens the red west, gains new ground.

What disarray of an irresistible weather damps the fag-end
Of our day? And I bear it like a girl.
I am afire with its tears, my words have the asperity of tears,
I am it would seem an acceptable tube; and therefore
While time is, let me be used.
And therefore not the miserable managements,
It is not the infringements on dusty plains
Of a corrupted oriental cavalry, it is not
The caballing of the monied men, and not
The refuse and rejected offal of strolling players, nor the
    hazards
Of a den of outlaws upon a doubtful frontier nor even
My own colloquies at dawn with deploring fields,
Will seduce me (I hope) or silence me. I hope my unhappy
    blood
And its favourite fever, may be given the grace
To give the truth my voice, truth to my voice, and may
The rich web so establish, while words are, while time is.

Autumn Journey

    I saw from the gliding train
    A yellow birch in the woods below,
    And the dark pines close in again,
    And thought of dry leaves falling slow
    Under the cold cloud-shadows,
    Horses of shadow, loosed in dreams;
    And of the Snow Queen, pale and fair,

And Gerda looking for her Kay,
Poor Gerda, when she met the crow
Who led her in by the back way:
So, as they climbed the castle stair
To reach the bedroom where he lay,
Dark horses plunged like shadows,
Long-legged on the wall, in dreams;
And Gerda, while her heart beat fast,
Came where he slept, half turned away,
And called him, and the dreams rushed past,
And he awoke, and was not Kay.

ROBERT LOWELL

The Flaw

A seal swims like a poodle through the sheet
of blinding salt. A country graveyard, here
and there a rock, and here and there a pine,
throbs on the essence of the gasoline.
Some mote, some eye-flaw, wobbles in the heat,
hair-thin, hair-dark, the fragment of a hair—

a noose, a question? All is possible;
if there's free will, it's something like this hair,
inside my eye, outside my eye, yet free,
airless as grace, if the good God . . . I see.
Our bodies quiver. In this rustling air,
all's possible, all's unpredictable.

Old wives and husbands! Look, their gravestones wait
in couples with the names and half the date—
one future and one freedom. In a flash,

I see us whiten into skeletons,
our eager, sharpened cries, a pair of stones,
cutting like shark-fins through the boundless wash.

Two walking cobwebs, almost bodiless,
crossed paths here once, kept house, and lay in beds.
Your fingertips once touched my fingertips
and set us tingling through a thousand threads.
Poor pulsing *Fête Champêtre!* The summer slips
between our fingers into nothingness.

We too lean forward, as the heat waves roll
over our bodies, grown insensible,
ready to dwindle off into the soul,
two motes or eye-flaws, the invisible . . .
Hope of the hopeless launched and cast adrift
on the great flaw that gives the final gift.

Dear Figure curving like a questionmark,
how will you hear my answer in the dark?

THEODORE ROETHKE

Cuttings

Sticks-in-a-drowse droop over sugary loam,
Their intricate stem-fur dries;
But still the delicate slips keep coaxing up water;
The small cells bulge;

One nub of growth
Nudges a sand-crumb loose,
Pokes through a musty sheath
Its pale tendrilous horn.

DELMORE SCHWARTZ

Do the Others Speak of Me
Mockingly, Maliciously?

*"As in water face answereth to face, so the heart of
man to man."*

Do they whisper behind my back? Do they speak
Of my clumsiness? Do they laugh at me,
Mimicking my gestures, retailing my shame?
I'll whirl about, denounce them, saying
That they are shameless, they are treacherous,
No more my friends, nor will I once again
Never, amid a thousand meetings in the street,
Recognize their faces, take their hands,
Not for our common love or old times' sake:
They whispered behind my back, they mimicked me.

I know the reason why, I too have done this,
Cruel for wit's sake, behind my dear friend's back,
And to amuse betrayed his private love,
His nervous shame, her habit, and their weaknesses;
I have mimicked them, I have been treacherous,
For wit's sake, to amuse, because their being weighed
Too grossly for a time, to be superior,
To flatter the listeners by this, the intimate,
Betraying the intimate, but for the intimate,
To free myself of friendship's necessity,
Fearing from time to time that they would hear,
Denounce me and reject me, say once for all
That they would never meet me, take my hands,
Speaking for old times' sake and our common love.

What an unheard-of thing it is, in fine,
To love another and equally be loved!
What sadness and what joy! How cruel it is
That pride and wit distort the heart of man,
How vain, how sad, what cruelty, what need,
For this is true and sad, that I need them
And they need me. What can we do? We need
Each other's clumsiness, each other's wit,
Each other's company and our own pride. I need
My face unshamed, I need my wit, I cannot
Turn away. We know our clumsiness,
Our weakness, our necessities, we cannot
Forget our pride, our faces, our common love.

ELIZABETH BISHOP

*Visits to St. Elizabeths**

1950

This is the house of Bedlam.

This is the man
that lies in the house of Bedlam.

This is the time
of the tragic man
that lies in the house of Bedlam.

This is a wristwatch
telling the time

---

* Where Ezra Pound was confined after World War II (Ed.).

of the talkative man
that lies in the house of Bedlam.

This is a sailor
wearing the watch
that tells the time
of the honored man
that lies in the house of Bedlam.

This is the roadstead all of board
reached by the sailor
wearing the watch
that tells the time
of the old, brave man
that lies in the house of Bedlam.

These are the years and the walls of the ward,
the winds and clouds of the sea of board
sailed by the sailor
wearing the watch
that tells the time
of the cranky man
that lies in the house of Bedlam.

This is a Jew in a newspaper hat
that dances weeping down the ward
over the creaking sea of board
beyond the sailor
winding his watch
that tells the time
of the cruel man
that lies in the house of Bedlam.

This is a world of books gone flat.
This is a Jew in a newspaper hat
that dances weeping down the ward
over the creaking sea of board
of the batty sailor
that winds his watch
that tells the time

of the busy man
that lies in the house of Bedlam.

This is a boy that pats the floor
to see if the world is there, is flat,
for the widowed Jew in the newspaper hat
that dances weeping down the ward
waltzing the length of a weaving board
by the silent sailor
that hears his watch
that ticks the time
of the tedious man
that lies in the house of Bedlam.

These are the years and the walls and the door
that shut on a boy that pats the floor
to feel if the world is there and flat.
This is a Jew in a newspaper hat
that dances joyfully down the ward
into the parting seas of board
past the staring sailor
that shakes his watch
that tells the time
of the poet, the man
that lies in the house of Bedlam.

This is the soldier home from the war.
These are the years and the walls and the door
that shut on a boy that pats the floor
to see if the world is round or flat.
This is a Jew in a newspaper hat
that dances carefully down the ward,
walking the plank of a coffin board
with the crazy sailor
that shows his watch
that tells the time
of the wretched man
that lies in the house of Bedlam.

~~~~~~

JAMES AGEE

~~~~~~~~~~~~~~~~~~~~~~~~~~

Variation 4

Where now the lizard and the rinded snake
That skipped and slurred their lengths and lusted in the heat?
Where the lean bugs that on the water break
Their rapid dances and each other eat?

The lithe-tongued butterfly where now is he
That chanced his bright wings on the unequal air?
Where the mean hornet and the sweet-groined bee:
Now they are under night how may these bloodless fare?

The reptile's eye is blue: the thready fly
Stands on the skin of water, he is well:
The tongue is furled and the fair dust not flawed and the
    wings shut high:
The stout bee grumbles in his paper cell:

"No doubt left . . ."

No doubt left. Enough deceiving.
Now I know you do not love.
Now you know I do not love.
Now we know we do not love.
No more doubt. No more deceiving.

Yet there is pity in us for each other
And better times are almost fresh as true.
The dog returns. And the man to his mother.
And tides. And you to me. And I to you.

And we are cowardly kind the cruellest way,
Feeling the cliff unmorsel from our heels
And knowing balance gone, we smile, and stay
A little, whirling our arms like desperate wheels.

Lullaby

Sleep, child, lie quiet, let be:
Now like a still wind, a great tree,
Night upon this city moves
Like leaves, our hungers and our loves.
 Sleep, rest easy, while you may.
 Soon it is day.

And elsewhere likewise love is stirred;
Elsewhere the speechless song is heard:
Wherever children sleep or wake,
Souls are lifted, hearts break.
 Sleep, be careless while you can.
 Soon you are man.

And everywhere good men contrive
Good reasons not to be alive.
And even should they build their best
No man could bear tell you the rest.
 Sleep child, for your parents' sake.
 Soon you must wake.

RANDALL JARRELL

In Montecito

In a fashionable suburb of Santa Barbara,
Montecito, there visited me one night at midnight
A scream with breasts. As it hung there in the sweet air
That was always the right temperature, the contractors
Who had undertaken to dismantle it, stripped off
The lips, let the air out of the breasts.

                              People disappear

Even in Montecito. Greenie Taliaferro,
In her white maillot, her good figure almost firm,
Her old pepper-and-salt hair stripped by the hairdresser
To nothing and dyed platinum—Greenie has left her Bentley.
They have thrown away her electric toothbrush, someone else
    slips
The key into the lock of her safety-deposit box
At the Crocker-Anglo Bank; her seat at the cricket matches
Is warmed by buttocks less delectable than hers.
Greenie's girdle is empty.

                     A scream hangs there in the night:
They strip off the lips, let the air out of the breasts,
And Greenie has gone into the Greater Montecito
That surrounds Montecito like the echo of a scream.

WELDON KEES

The Beach in August

The day the fat woman
In the bright blue bathing suit
Walked into the water and died,
I thought about the human
Condition. Pieces of old fruit
Came in and were left by the tide.

What I thought about the human
Condition was this: old fruit
Comes in and is left, and dries
In the sun. Another fat woman
In a dull green bathing suit
Dives into the water and dies.
The pulmotors glisten. It is noon.

We dry and die in the sun
While the seascape arranges old fruit,
Coming in with the tide, glistening
At noon. A woman, moderately stout,
In a nondescript bathing suit,
Swims to a pier. A tall woman
Steps toward the sea. One thinks about the human
Condition. The tide goes in and goes out.

Aspects of Robinson

Robinson at cards at the Algonquin; a thin
Blue light comes down once more outside the blinds.
Gray men in overcoats are ghosts blown past the door.
The taxis streak the avenues with yellow, orange, and red.
This is Grand Central, Mr. Robinson.

Robinson on a roof above the Heights; the boats
Mourn like the lost. Water is slate, far down.
Through sounds of ice cubes dropped in glass, an osteopath,
Dressed for the links, describes an old Intourist tour.
—Here's where old Gibbons jumped from, Robinson.
Robinson walking in the Park, admiring the elephant.
Robinson buying the *Tribune,* Robinson buying the *Times.*
    Robinson
Saying, "Hello. Yes, this is Robinson. Sunday
At five? I'd love to. Pretty well. And you?"
Robinson alone at Longchamps, staring at the wall.

Robinson afraid, drunk, sobbing. Robinson
In bed with a Mrs. Morse. Robinson at home;
Decisions: Toynbee or luminol? Where the sun
Shines, Robinson in flowered trunks, eyes toward
The breakers. Where the night ends, Robinson in East Side
    bars.

Robinson in Glen plaid jacket, Scotch-grain shoes,
Black four-in-hand and oxford button-down,
The jeweled and silent watch that winds itself, the brief-
Case, covert topcoat, clothes for spring, all covering
His sad and usual heart, dry as a winter leaf.

Dog

To Vincent McHugh

"This night is monstrous winter when the rats
Swarm in great packs along the waterfront,
When midnight closes in and takes away your name.
And it was Rover, Ginger, Laddie, Prince;
My pleasure hambones. Donned a collar once
With golden spikes, the darling of a cultured home
Somewhere between the harbor and the heights, uptown.
Or is this something curs with lathered mouths invent?
They had a little boy I would have bitten, had I dared.
They threw great bones out on the balcony.
But where? I pant at every door tonight.

I knew this city once the way I know those lights
Blinking in chains along the other side,
These streets that hold the odors of my kind.
But now, my bark a ghost in this strange scentless air,
I am no growling cicerone or cerberus
But wreckage for the pound, snuffling in shame
All cold-nosed toward identity.—Rex? Ginger? No.
A sort of panic jabbering inside begins.
Wild for my shadow in this vacantness,
I can at least run howling toward the bankrupt lights
Into the traffic where bones, cats, and masters swarm,
And where my name must be."

The Coming of the Plague

September was when it began.
Locusts dying in the fields; our dogs
Silent, moving like shadows on a wall;
And strange worms crawling; flies of a kind
We had never seen before; huge vineyard moths;
Badgers and snakes, abandoning

Their holes in the field; the fruit gone rotten;
Queer fungi sprouting; the fields and woods
Covered with spiderwebs; black vapors
Rising from the earth—all these,
And more, began that fall. Ravens flew round
The hospital in pairs. Where there was water,
We could hear the sound of beating clothes
All through the night. We could not count
All the miscarriages, the quarrels, the jealousies.
And one day in a field I saw
A swarm of frogs, swollen and hideous,
Hundreds upon hundreds, sitting on each other,
Huddled together, silent, ominous,
And heard the sound of rushing wind.

JOHN BERRYMAN

Henry's Confession

Nothin very bad happen to me lately.
How you explain that?—I explain that, Mr Bones,
terms o' your bafflin odd sobriety.
Sober as man can get, no girls, no telephones,
what could happen bad to Mr Bones?
—*If* life is a handkerchief sandwich,

in a modesty of death I join my father
who dared so long agone leave me.
A bullet on a concrete stoop
close by a smothering southern sea
spreadeagled on an island, by my knee.
—You is from hunger, Mr Bones,

I offers you this handkerchief, now set
your left foot by my right foot,
shoulder to shoulder, all that jazz,
arm in arm, by the beautiful sea,
hum a little, Mr Bones.
—I saw nobody coming, so I went instead.

185

The drill was after or is into him.
Whirr went a bite. He should not feel this bad.
A truly first-class drill.
Nothing distinctly hurts. It reminds him.
—Like it makes you blink, Mr Bones, of was & will?
—Very much so.

Conundrums at the gum-line.
I've been jumpy for the last 37 years,
pal.
The more I lessen to, the bore I hears.
Drugging & prodding me! 'His Majesty,
the body.'

'Gynecomastia' the surgeon called,
'the man is old & bald
and has habits. In this circumstance
I cannot save him.' The older you get, at once
the better death looks and
the more fearful & intolerable.

263

You couldn't bear to grow old, but we grow old.
Our differences accumulate. Our skin
tightens or droops: it alters.
Take courage, things are not what they have been

and they will never again. Hot hearts grow cold,
the rush to the surface falters,

secretive grows the disappearing soul
learned & uncertain, young again
but not in the same way:
Heraclitus had a wise word here to say,
which I forget. We wake & blunder on,
wiser, on the whole,

but not more accurate. Leave that to the young,
grope forward, toward where no one else has been
which is our privilege.
Besides, you gave up early in our age
which is your privilege, from Chatterton
to the bitter & present scene.

149

This world is gradually becoming a place
where I do not care to be any more. Can Delmore die?
I don't suppose
in all them years a day went ever by
without a loving thought for him. Welladay.
In the brightness of his promise,

unstained, I saw him thro' the mist of the actual
blazing with insight, warm with gossip
thro' all our Harvard years
when both of us were just becoming known
I got him out of a police-station once, in Washington, t
     world is *tref*
and grief too astray for tears.

I imagine you have heard the terrible news,
that Delmore Schwartz is dead, miserably & alone
in New York: he sang me a song

'I am the Brooklyn poet Delmore Schwartz
Harms & the child I sing, two parents' torts'
when he was young & gift-strong.

Herbert Park, Dublin

Were you góod tó him? He was not to you:
I know: it was in his later years
when he could not be good to anybody:
pain & disorder, baseless fears,
malign influences
ruled his descending star,

which crowds today my thought from observation
of this most beautiful of parks since Bombay
on this éxquisite October Sunday,
the great bright green spaces under the fine sun,
children & ducks & dogs, two superb elms,
the scene Henry overwhelms.

We traverse a trellis, magisterial.
A little is rolling over & over   on the turf, my own.
That dreadful small-hours hotel death mars all.
Did you leave him all alone,
to that end? or did he leave you, to seek
frailty & tremor, obsessed, mad & weak?

382

At Henry's bier let some thing fall out well:
enter there none who somewhat has to sell,
the music ancient & gradual,
the voices solemn but the grief subdued,
no hairy jokes but everybody's mood
subdued, subdued,

until the Dancer comes, in a short short dress
hair black & long & loose, dark dark glasses,
uptilted face,
pallor & strangeness, the music changes
to 'Give!' & 'Ow!' and how! the music changes,
she kicks a backward limb

on tiptoe, pirouettes, & she is free
to the knocking music, sails, dips, & suddenly
returns to the terrible gay
occasion hopeless & mad, she weaves, it's hell,
she flings to her head a leg, bobs, all is well,
she dances Henry away.

SYLVIA PLATH

Last Words

I do not want a plain box, I want a sarcophagus
with tigery stripes, and a face on it
round as the moon, to stare up.
I want to be looking at them when they come
picking among the dumb minerals, the roots.
I see them already—the pale, star-distance faces.
Now they are nothing, they are not even babies.
I imagine them without fathers or mothers, like the first gods.
They will wonder if I was important.
I should sugar and preserve my days like fruit!
My mirror is clouding over—
a few more breaths, and it will reflect nothing at all.
The flowers and the faces whiten to a sheet.

I do not trust the spirit. It escapes like steam
in dreams, through mouth-hole or eye-hole. I can't stop it.
One day it won't come back. Things aren't like that.
They stay, their little particular lusters
warmed by much handling. They almost purr.
When the soles of my feet grow cold,
the blue eye of my turquoise will comfort me.
Let me have my copper cooking pots, let my rouge pots
bloom about me like night flowers, with a good smell.
They will roll me up in bandages, they will store my heart
under my feet in a neat parcel.
I shall hardly know myself. It will be dark,
and the shine of these small things sweeter than the face of
    Ishtar.

Lady Lazarus

I have done it again.
One year in every ten
I manage it——

A sort of walking miracle, my skin
Bright as a Nazi lampshade,
My right foot

A paperweight,
My face a featureless, fine
Jew linen.

Peel off the napkin
O my enemy.
Do I terrify?——

The nose, the eye pits, the full set of teeth?
The sour breath
Will vanish in a day.

Soon, soon the flesh
The grave cave ate will be
At home on me

And I a smiling woman.
I am only thirty.
And like the cat I have nine times to die.

This is Number Three.
What a trash
To annihilate each decade.

What a million filaments.
The peanut-crunching crowd
Shoves in to see

Them unwrap me hand and foot——
The big strip tease.
Gentleman, ladies,

These are my hands,
My knees.
I may be skin and bone,

I may be Japanese.
The first time it happened I was ten.
It was an accident.

The second time I meant
To last it out and not come back at all.
I rocked shut

As a seashell.
They had to call and call
And pick the worms off me like sticky pearls.

Dying
Is an art, like everything else.
I do it exceptionally well.

I do it so it feels like hell.
I do it so it feels real.
I guess you could say I've a call.

It's easy enough to do it in a cell.
It's easy enough to do it and stay put.
It's the theatrical

Comeback in broad day
To the same place, the same face, the same brute
Amused shout:

"A miracle!"
That knocks me out.
There is a charge

For the eyeing of my scars, there is a charge
For the hearing of my heart——
It really goes.

And there is a charge, a very large charge,
For a word or a touch
Or a bit of blood

Or a piece of my hair or my clothes.
So, so, Herr Doktor.
So, Herr Enemy.

I am your opus,
I am your valuable,
The pure gold baby

That melts to a shriek.
I turn and burn.
Do not think I underestimate your great concern.

Ash, ash——
You poke and stir.
Flesh, bone, there is nothing there——

A cake of soap,
A wedding ring,
A gold filling.

Edge

The woman is perfected.
Her dead

Body wears the smile of accomplishment,
The illusion of a Greek necessity

Flows in the scrolls of her toga,
Her bare

Feet seem to be saying:
We have come so far, it is over.

Each dead child coiled, a white serpent,
One at each little

Pitcher of milk, now empty.
She has folded

Them back into her body as petals
Of a rose close when the garden

Stiffens and odours bleed
From the sweet, deep throats of the night flower.

The moon has nothing to be sad about,
Staring from her hood of bone.

She is used to this sort of thing.
Her blacks crackle and drag.

~~~~~~~~~~~~~~~~~~~~~~~~~~~~~~~~~

MAY SWENSON

~~~~~~~~~~~~~~~~~~~~~

The Key to Everything

Is there anything I can do
or has everything been done
or do
you prefer somebody else to do
it or don't
you trust me to do
it right or is it hopeless and no one can do
a thing or do
you suppose I don't
really want to do
it and am just saying that or don't
you hear me at all or what?

You're
waiting for
the right person the doctor or
the nurse the father or
the mother or
the person with the name you keep
mumbling in your sleep
that no one ever heard of there's no one
named that really
except yourself maybe

If I knew what your name was I'd
prove it's your
own name spelled backwards or
twisted in some way the one you
keep mumbling but you
won't tell me your

name or
don't you know it
yourself that's it
of course you've
forgotten or
never quite knew it or
weren't willing to believe it

Then there *is* something I
can do I
can find your name for you
that's the key to everything once you'd
repeat it clearly you'd
get up and walk knowing where you're
going where you
came from

And you'd
love me
after that or would you
hate me?
no once you'd
get there you'd
remember and love me
of course I'd
be gone by then I'd
be far away

STEVIE SMITH

Not Waving but Drowning

Nobody heard him, the dead man,
But still he lay moaning:
I was much further out than you thought
And not waving but drowning.

Poor chap, he always loved larking
And now he's dead
It must have been too cold for him his heart gave way,
They said.

Oh, no no no, it was too cold always
(Still the dead one lay moaning)
I was much too far out all my life
And not waving but drowning.

Private Means Is Dead

Private Means is dead
God rest his soul, officers and fellow-rankers said.

Captive Good, attending Captain Ill
Can tell us quite a lot about the Captain, if he will.

Major Portion
Is a disingenuous person
And as for Major Operation well I guess
We all know what his reputation is.

The crux and Colonel
Of the whole matter
(As you may read in the Journal
If it's not tattered)

Lies in the Generals Collapse, Debility, Panic and Uproa
Who are too old in any case to go to the War.

Mother, Among the Dustbins

Mother, among the dustbins and the manure
I feel the measure of my humanity, an allure
As of the presence of God.   I am sure

In the dustbins, in the manure, in the cat at play,
Is the presence of God, in a sure way
He moves there.   Mother, what do you say?

I too have felt the presence of God in the broom
I hold, in the cobwebs in the room,
But most of all in the silence of the tomb.

Ah! but that thought that informs the hope of our kind
Is but an empty thing, what lies behind?—
Naught but the vanity of a protesting mind

That would not die.   This is the thought that bounces
Within a conceited head and trounces
Inquiry.   Man is most frivolous when he pronounces.

Well Mother, I shall continue to think as I do,
And I think you would be wise to do so too,
Can you question the folly of man in the creation of God
     Who are you?

The Failed Spirit

To those who are isolate
War comes, promising respite,
Making what seems to be up to the moment the most
    successful endeavour
Against the fort of the failed spirit that is alone for ever.
Spurious failed spirit, adamantine wasture,
Crop, spirit, crop thy stony pasture!

Harold's Leap

Harold, are you asleep?
Harold, I remember your leap,
It may have killed you
But it was a brave thing to do.
Two promontories ran high into the sky,
He leapt from one rock to the other
And fell to the sea's smother.
Harold was always afraid to climb high,
But something urged him on,
He felt he should try.
I would not say that he was wrong,
Although he succeeded in doing nothing but die.
Would you?
Ever after that steep
Place was called Harold's Leap.
It was a brave thing to do.

KINGSLEY AMIS

The Voice of Authority: A Language Game

Do this. Don't move. O'Grady says do this,
You get a move on, see, do what I say.
Look lively when I say O'Grady says.

Say this. Shut up. O'Grady says say this,
You talk fast without thinking what to say.
What goes is what I say O'Grady says.

Or rather let me put the point like this:
O'Grady says what goes is what I say
O'Grady says; that's what O'Grady says.

By substituting you can shorten this,
Since any god you like will do to say
The things you like, that's what O'Grady says.

The harm lies not in that, but in that this
Progression's first and last terms are I say
O'Grady says, not just O'Grady says.

Yet it's O'Grady must be out of this
Before what we say goes, not what we say
O'Grady says. Or so O'Grady says.

Coming of Age

Twenty years ago he slipped into town.
A spiritual secret agent; took
Rooms right in the cathedral close; wrote down
Verbatim all their direst idioms;
Made phonetic transcripts in his black book;
Mimicked their dress, their gestures as they sat
Chaffering and chaffing in the Grand Hotel;
Infiltrated their glass-and-plastic homes,
Watched from the inside; then—his deadliest blow—
Went and married one of them (what about that?);
At the first christening played his part so well
That he started living it from then on,
His trick of camouflage no longer a trick.
Isn't it the spy's rarest triumph to grow
Indistinguishable from the spied upon,
The stick insect's to become a stick?

A Note on Wyatt

See her come bearing down, a tidy craft!
Gaily her topsails bulge, her sidelights burn!
There's jigging in her rigging fore and aft,
And beauty's self, not name, limned on her stern.

See at her head the Jolly Roger flutters!
"God, is she fully manned? If she's one short . . ."
Cadet, bargee, longshoreman, shellback mutters;
Drowned is reason that should me comfort.

But habit, like a cork, rides the dark flood,
And, like a cork, keeps her in walls of glass;
Faint legacies of brine tingle my blood,
The tide-wind's fading echoes, as I pass.

Now, jolly ship, sign on a jolly crew:
God bless you, dear, and all who sail in you.

PHILIP LARKIN

Toads

Why should I let the toad *work*
   Squat on my life?
Can't I use my wit as a pitchfork
   And drive the brute off?

Six days of the week it soils
   With its sickening poison—
Just for paying a few bills!
   That's out of proportion.

Lots of folk live on their wits:
   Lecturers, lispers,
Losels, loblolly-men, louts—
   They don't end as paupers;

Lots of folk live up lanes
   With fires in a bucket,
Eat windfalls and tinned sardines—
   They seem to like it.

Their nippers have got bare feet,
   Their unspeakable wives
Are skinny as whippets—and yet
   No one actually *starves*.

Ah, were I courageous enough
   To shout *Stuff your pension!*
But I know, all too well, that's the stuff
   That dreams are made on:

For something sufficiently toad-like
    Squats in me, too;
Its hunkers are heavy as hard luck,
    And cold as snow,

And will never allow me to blarney
    My way to getting
The fame and the girl and the money
    All at one sitting.

Mr Bleaney

'This was Mr Bleaney's room. He stayed
The whole time he was at the Bodies, till
They moved him.' Flowered curtains, thin and frayed,
Fall to within five inches of the sill,

Whose window shows a strip of building land,
Tussocky, littered. 'Mr Bleaney took
My bit of garden properly in hand.'
Bed, upright chair, sixty-watt bulb, no hook

Behind the door, no room for books or bags—
'I'll take it.' So it happens that I lie
Where Mr Bleaney lay, and stub my fags
On the same saucer-souvenir, and try

Stuffing my ears with cotton-wool, to drown
The jabbering set he egged her on to buy.
I know his habits—what time he came down,
His preference for sauce to gravy, why

He kept on plugging at the four aways—
Likewise their yearly frame: the Frinton folk
Who put him up for summer holidays,
And Christmas at his sister's house in Stoke.

But if he stood and watched the frigid wind
Tousling the clouds, lay on the fusty bed
Telling himself that this was home, and grinned,
And shivered, without shaking off the dread

That how we live measures our own nature,
And at his age having no more to show
Than one hired box should make him pretty sure
He warranted no better, I don't know.

Toads Revisited

Walking around in the park
Should feel better than work:
The lake, the sunshine,
The grass to lie on,

Blurred playground noises
Beyond black-stockinged nurses—
Not a bad place to be.
Yet it doesn't suit me,

Being one of the men
You meet of an afternoon:
Palsied old step-takers,
Hare-eyed clerks with the jitters,

Waxed-fleshed out-patients
Still vague from accidents,
And characters in long coats
Deep in the litter-baskets—

All dodging the toad work
By being stupid or weak.
Think of being them!
Hearing the hours chime,

Watching the bread delivered,
The sun by clouds covered,
The children going home;
Think of being them,

Turning over their failures
By some bed of lobelias,
Nowhere to go but indoors,
No friends but empty chairs—

No, give me my in-tray,
My loaf-haired secretary,
My shall-I-keep-the-call-in-Sir:
What else can I answer,

When the lights come on at four
At the end of another year?
Give me your arm, old toad;
Help me down Cemetery Road.

DONALD DAVIE

Time Passing, Beloved

Time passing, and the memories of love
Coming back to me, carissima, no more mockingly
Than ever before; time passing, unslackening,
Unhastening, steadily; and no more
Bitterly, beloved, the memories of love
Coming into the shore.

How will it end? Time passing, and our passages of love
As ever, beloved, blind

As ever before; time binding, unbinding
About us; and yet to remember
Never less chastening, nor the flame of love
Less like an ember.

What will become of us? Time
Passing, beloved, and we in a sealed
Assurance unassailed
By memory. How can it end,
This siege of a shore that no misgivings have steeled,
No doubts defend?

The Mushroom Gatherers

After Mickiewicz

Strange walkers! See their processional
Perambulations under low boughs,
The birches white, and the green turf under.
These should be ghosts by moonlight wandering.

Their attitudes strange; the human tree
Slowly revolves on its bole. All around
Downcast looks; and the direct dreamer
Treads out in trance his lane, unwavering.

Strange decorum: so prodigal of bows,
Yet lost in thought and self-absorbed, they meet
Impassively, without acknowledgment.
A courteous nation, but unsociable.

Field full of folk, in their immunity
From human ills, crestfallen and serene,
Who would have thought these shades our lively friends?
Surely these acres are Elysian Fields.

The Hill Field

Look there! What a wheaten
Half-loaf, halfway to bread,
A cornfield is, that is eaten
Away, and harvested:

How like a loaf, where the knife
Has cut and come again,
Jagged where the farmer's wife
Has served the farmer's men,

That steep field is, where the reaping
Has only just begun
On a wedge-shaped front, and the creeping
Steel edges glint in the sun.

See the cheese-like shape it is taking,
The sliced-off walls of the wheat
And the cheese-mite reapers making
Inroads there, in the heat?

It is Brueghel or Samuel Palmer,
Some painter, coming between
My eye and the truth of a farmer,
So massively sculpts the scene.

The sickles of poets dazzle
These eyes that were filmed from birth;
And the miller comes with an easel
To grind the fruits of earth.

Or, Solitude

A farm boy lost in the snow
Rides his good horse, Madrone,
Through Iowan snows for ever
And is called "alone".

Because gone from the land
Are the boys who knew it best
Or best expressed it, gone
To Boston or Out West,

And the breed of the horse Madrone,
With its bronco strain, is strange
To the broken sod of Iowa
That used to be its range,

The transcendental nature
Of poetry, how I need it!
And yet it was for years
What I refused to credit.

THOMAS KINSELLA

Wormwood

I have dreamt it again: standing suddenly still
In a thicket, among wet trees, stunned, minutely
Shuddering, hearing a wooden echo escape.

A mossy floor, almost colourless, disappears
In depths of rain among the tree shapes.
I am straining, tasting that echo a second longer.

If I can hold it . . . familiar if I can hold it . . .
A black tree with a double trunk—two trees
Grown into one—throws up its blurred branches.

The two trunks in their infinitesimal dance of growth
Have turned completely about one another, their join
A slowly twisted scar . . . that I recognize . . .

A quick arc flashes sidewise in the air,
A heavy blade in flight. A wooden stroke:
Iron sinks in the gasping core.
                              I will dream again.

Fire and Ice

Two creatures face each other, fixed in song,
Satyr and nymph, across the darkening brain.
I dream of reason and the first grows strong,
Drunk as a whirlwind on the sweating grain;
I dream of drunkenness and, freed from strain,
The second murmurs like a fingered gong;
I sink beneath the dream: his words grow sane,
Her pupils glow with pleasure all night long.

At the Heart

Heraldic, hatched in gold, a sacred tree
Stands absorbed, tinkering with the slight
Thrumming of birds, the flicker of energy
Thrown and caught, the blows and burdens of flight.
Roots deepen; disciplines proliferate
And wings more fragile are brought into play.
Timber matures, the game grows nobler, yet
Not one has sped direct as appetite.

CHARLES TOMLINSON

Through Closed Eyes

Light burns through blood:
a shuttering of shadow brings
the cloud behind the retina, and through
a double darkness, climbs
by the ascent the image is descending
a faceless possible, a form
seeking its sustenance in space.

The Fox

When I saw the fox, it was kneeling
in snow: there was nothing to confess
that, tipped on its broken forepaws
the thing was dead—save for its stillness.

A drift, confronting me, leaned down
across the hill-top field. The wind
had scarped it into a pennine wholly of snow, and
where did the hill go now?

There was no way round:
I drew booted legs
back out of it, took to my tracks again,
but already a million blown snow-motes were
    flowing and filling them in.

Domed at the summit, then tapering,
the drift still mocked
my mind as if the whole
fox-infested hill were the skull of a fox.

Scallops and dips
of pure pile rippled and shone, but what
should I do with such beauty
eyed by that?

It was like clambering between its white temples
as the crosswind tore
at one's knees, and each
missed step was a plunge at the hill's blinding interior.

Palm of the Hand

(A version after Rilke)

Palm of the hand. Sole, that no longer walks
except on touch. It is exposed:
a mirror that will give
welcome to heavenly highways
which themselves are fugitive.
Transformer of all turnings,
it has learnt to go
on water, when it scoops it in, to follow
the fountain as it springs.
It enters other hands,
changes its like to landscape,
wanders and returns
in them, its shape
filling them with arrival.

Observation of Facts

Facts have no eyes. One must
Surprise them, as one surprises a tree
By regarding its (shall I say?)
Facets of copiousness.

The tree stands.

The house encloses.

The room flowers.

These are fact stripped of imagination:
Their relation is mutual.

A dryad is a sort of chintz curtain
Between myself and a tree.
The tree stands: or does not stand:
As I draw, or remove the curtain.

The house encloses: or fails to signify
As being bodied over against one,
As something one has to do with.

The room flowers once one has introduced
Mental fibre beneath its elegance,
A rough pot or two, outweighing
The persistence of frippery
In lampshades or wallpaper.

Style speaks what was seen,
Or it conceals the observation
Behind the observer: a voice
Wearing a ruff.

Those facets of copiousness which I proposed
Exist, do so when we have silenced ourselves.

THOM GUNN

The Secret Sharer

Over the ankles in snow and numb past pain
I stared up at my window three stories high:
From a white street unconcerned as a dead eye,
I patiently called my name again and again.

The curtains were lit, through glass were lit by doubt
And there was I, within the room alone.
In the empty wind I stood and shouted on:
But O, what if the strange head should peer out?

Suspended taut between two equal fears
I was like to be torn apart by their strong pull:
What, I asked, if I never hear my call?
And what if it reaches my insensitive ears?

Fixed in my socket of thought I saw them move
Aside, I saw that some uncertain hand
Had touched the curtains. Mine, I wondered? And,
At this instant, the wind turned in its groove.

The wind turns in its groove and I am here
Lying in bed, the snow and street outside;
Fire-glow still reassuring; dark defied.
The wind turns in its groove: I am still there.

The First Man

The present is a secure place to inhabit,
The past being fallen from the mind, the future
A repetition, only, with variations:
The same mouse on its haunches, nibbling, absorbed,
Another piece of root between the forefeet
Slender as wishbones; the woodlice, silvery balls;
The leaves still falling in vestiges of light.

Is he a man? If man is cogitation,
This is at most a rudimentary man,
An unreflecting organ of perception;
Slow as a bull, in moving; yet, in taking,
Quick as an adder. He does not dream at night.

Echo is in the past, the snow long past,
The year has recovered and put forth many times.

He is bent, looks smaller, and is furred, it seems.
Mole-like he crouches over mounds of dirt,
Sifting. His eyes have sunk behind huge brows.
His nostrils twitch, distinguishing one by one
The smells of the unseen that blend to make
The black smell of the earth, smell of the Mother,
Smell of her food: pale tender smell of worms,
Tough sweet smell of her roots. He is a nose.
He picks through the turned earth, and eats. A mouth.

If he is man, he is the first man lurking
In a thicket of time. The mesh of green grows tighter.
There is yew, and oak picked out with mistletoe.
Watch, he is darkening in the heavy shade
Of trunks that thicken in the ivy's grip.

In the Tank

A man sat in the felon's tank, alone,
Fearful, ungrateful, in a cell for two.
And from his metal bunk, the lower one,
He studied where he was, as felons do.

The cell was clean and cornered, and contained
A bowl, grey gritty soap, and paper towels,
A mattress lumpy and not over-stained,
Also a toilet, for the felon's bowels.

He could see clearly all there was to see,
And later when the lights flicked off at nine
He saw as clearly all there was to see:
An order without colour, bulk, or line.

And then he knew exactly where he sat.
For though the total riches could not fail
—Red weathered brick, fountains, wisteria—yet
Still they contained the silence of a jail,

The jail contained a tank, the tank contained
A box, a mere suspension, at the centre,
Where there was nothing left to understand,
And where he must re-enter and re-enter.

D. J. ENRIGHT

Sightseeing

Along the long wide temple wall
Extends a large and detailed painting.

A demon's head, its mouth square open,
Inside the mouth a room of people squatting.

Its fangs the polished pillars of the room,
The crimson carpet of the floor its tongue.

Inside this room a painting on the wall,
A demon's head, its mouth square open.

Inside the mouth a room of people squatting,
Their faces blank, the artist did not care.

Inside that room a painting on the wall,
A demon's head, its mouth square open.

Somewhere you are squatting, somewhere there.
Imagination, like the eyes that strain

Against the wall, is happily too weak
To number all the jaws there are to slip.

The Poor Wake Up Quickly

Surprised at night,
The trishaw driver
Slithers from the carriage,
Hurls himself upon the saddle.

With what violence he peddles
Slapbang into the swarming night,
Neon skidding off his cheekbones!
Madly he makes away
In the wrong direction.
I tap his shoulder nervously.
Madly he turns about
Between the taxis and the trams,
Makes away electric-eyed
In another wrong direction.

How do I star in that opium dream?
A hulking red-faced ruffian
Who beats him on his bony back,
Cursing in the tongue of demons.
But when we're there
He grumbles mildly over his wage,
Like a sober man,
A man who has had no recent visions.
The poor wake up quickly.

The Burning of the Pipes

Bangkok, 1 July, 1959

Who would imagine they were government property?—
Wooden cylinders with collars of silver, coming
From China, brown and shiny with sweat and age.
Inside them were banks of dreams, shiny with
Newness, though doubtless of time-honoured stock.

They were easy to draw on: you pursed your lips
As if to suckle and sucked your breath as if to
Sigh: two skills which most of us have mastered.

The dreams themselves weren't government property.
Rather, the religion of the people. While the state
Took its tithes and the compliance of sleepers.
Now a strong government dispenses with compliance,
A government with rich friends has no need of tithes.

What acrid jinn was it that entered their flesh?
For some, a magic saucer, over green enamelled
Parks and lofty flat-faced city offices, to
Some new Tamerlane in his ticker-tape triumph—
Romantics! They had been reading books.
Others found the one dream left them: dreamless sleep.

As for us, perhaps we had eaten too much to dream,
To need to dream, I mean, or have to sleep.
For us, a moment of thinking our thoughts were viable,
And hope not a hopeless pipe-dream; for us
The gift of forgiveness for the hole in the road,
The dog we ran over on our way to bed.
Wasn't that something? The Chinese invented so much.

A surprise to find they were government property
—Sweat-brown bamboo with dull silver inlay—
As they blaze in thousands on a government bonfire,
In the government park, by government order!
The rice crop is expected to show an increase,
More volunteers for the army, and navy, and
Government service, and a decrease in petty crime.

Not the first time that fire destroys a dream.
Coca-cola sellers slither through the crowd; bats
Agitate among the rain-trees; flash-bulbs pop.
A holocaust of wooden legs—a miracle constated!
Rubbing his hands, the Marshal steps back from
The smoke, lost in a dream of strong government.

Sad, but they couldn't be beaten into TV sets;
As tourist souvenirs no self-respecting state
Could sponsor them, even at thirty dollars each.

Changing the Subject

I had suggested, in exasperation, that he find
    something other to write about
Than the moon, and flowers, and birds, and temples,
    and the bare hills of the once holy city—

People, I proposed, who bravely push their way
    through the leprous lakes of mud.
It was the wet season, rain upon spittle and urine,
    and I had been bravely pushing my way.

It happened my hard words chimed with a new slogan,
    a good idea, since ruined—
'Humanism'. So I helped on a fashion, another like
    mambo, French chanson, and learning Russian.

Now he comes back, my poet, in a different guise:
    the singer of those who sleep in the subway.
'Welcome you are,' his vagrants declaim to each other,
    'a comrade of the common fate.'

'Are they miners from Kyushu?' he asks, these 'hobos
    all in rags.' And adds that
'Broken bamboo baskets, their constant companions, watch
    loyally over their sleeping masters.'

Thus my friend. He asks me if he has passed the test,
    is he truly humanistic,
Will I write another article, about his change of heart?
    I try to think of the subway sleepers.

Who are indescribable. Have no wives or daughters to sell.
    Not the grain of faith that makes a beggar.

Have no words. No thing to express. No 'comrade'.
   Nothing so gratifying as a 'common fate'.

Their broken bamboo baskets are loyal because no one
   would wish to seduce them.
Their ochre skin still burns in its black nest, though a
   hundred changed poets decide to sing them.

'Are they miners from Kyushu?' Neither he nor I will
   ever dare to ask them.
For we know they are not really human, are as apt themes
   for verse as the moon and the bare hills.

Along the River

They had pulled her out of the river. She was dead,
Lying against the rhododendrons sewn with spider's thread.
An oldish woman, in a shabby dress, a straggling stocking,
A worn, despairing face. How could the old do such a thing?

Now forty years have passed. Again I recall that poor
Thing laid along the River Leam, and I look once more.

They have pulled her out of the river. She is dead,
Lying against the rhododendrons sewn with spider's thread.
A youngish woman, in a sodden dress, a straggling stocking,
A sad, appealing face. How can the young do such a thing?

RICHARD WILBUR

Piazza di Spagna,
Early Morning

I can't forget
How she stood at the top of that long marble stair
Amazed, and then with a sleepy pirouette
Went dancing slowly down to the fountain-quieted square;

Nothing upon her face
But some impersonal loneliness—not then a girl,
But as it were a reverie of the place,
A called-for falling glide and whirl;

As when a leaf, petal, or thin chip
Is drawn to the falls of a pool and, circling a moment above it,
Rides on over the lip—
Perfectly beautiful, perfectly ignorant of it.

The Undead

Even as children they were late sleepers,
Preferring their dreams, even when quick with monsters,
To the world with all its breakable toys,
Its compacts with the dying;

From the stretched arms of withered trees
They turned, fearing contagion of the mortal,
And even under the plums of summer
Drifted like winter moons.

Secret, unfriendly, pale, possessed
Of the one wish, the thirst for mere survival,
They came, as all extremists do
In time, to a sort of grandeur:

Now, to their Balkan battlements
Above the vulgar town of their first lives,
They rise at the moon's rising. Strange
That their utter self-concern

Should, in the end, have left them selfless:
Mirrors fail to perceive them as they float
Through the great hall and up the staircase;
Nor are the cobwebs broken.

Into the pallid night emerging,
Wrapped in their flapping capes, routinely maddened
By a wolf's cry, they stand for a moment
Stoking the mind's eye

With lewd thoughts of the pressed flowers
And bric-a-brac of rooms with something to lose,—
Of love-dismembered dolls, and children
Buried in quilted sleep.

Then they are off in a negative frenzy,
Their black shapes cropped into sudden bats
That swarm, burst, and are gone. Thinking
Of a thrush cold in the leaves

Who has sung his few summers truly,
Or an old scholar resting his eyes at last,
We cannot be much impressed with vampires,
Colorful though they are;

Nevertheless, their pain is real,
And requires our pity. Think how sad it must be
To thirst always for a scorned elixir,
The salt quotidian blood

Which, if mistrusted, has no savor;
To prey on life forever and not possess it,
    As rock-hollows, tide after tide,
        Glassily strand the sea.

The Lilacs

Those laden lilacs
           at the lawn's end
Came stark, spindly,
            and in staggered file,
Like walking wounded
            from the dead of winter.
We watched them waken
            in the brusque weather
To rot and rootbreak,
            to ripped branches,
And saw them shiver
            as the memory swept them
Of night and numbness
            and the taste of nothing.
Out of present pain
            and from past terror
Their bullet-shaped buds
            came quick and bursting,
As if they aimed
            to be open with us!

But the sun suddenly
            settled about them,
And green and grateful
            the lilacs grew,
Healed in that hush,
            that hospital quiet.
These lacquered leaves
            where the light paddles
And the big blooms
            buzzing among them

Have kept their counsel,
                        conveying nothing
Of their mortal message,
                        unless one should measure
The depth and dumbness
                        of death's kingdom
By the pure power
                        of this perfume.

Thyme Flowering Among Rocks

This, if Japanese,
Would represent grey boulders
Walloped by rough seas

So that, here or there,
The balked water tossed its froth
Straight into the air.

Here, where things are what
They are, it is thyme blooming,
Rocks, and nothing but—

Having, nonetheless,
Many small leaves implicit,
A green countlessness.

Crouching down, peering
Into perplexed recesses,
You find a clearing

Occupied by sun
Where, along prone, rachitic
Branches, one by one,

Pale stems arise, squared
In the manner of *Mentha*,
The oblong leaves paired.

One branch, in ending,
Lifts a little and begets
A straight-ascending

Spike, whorled with fine blue
Or purple trumpets, banked in
The leaf-axils. You

Are lost now in dense
Fact, fact which one might have thought
Hidden from the sense,

Blinking at detail
Peppery as this fragrance,
Lost to proper scale

As, in the motion
Of striped fins, a bathysphere
Forgets the ocean.

It makes the craned head
Spin. Unfathomed thyme! The world's
A dream, Basho said,

Not because that dream's
A falsehood, but because it's
Truer than it seems.

CHRISTOPHER MIDDLETON

Disturbing the Tarantula

The door a maze
of shadow, peach leaves
veining its wood colour,

and cobwebs broken
breathing ah ah
as it is pushed open—

two hands
at a ladder shook
free the tarantula, it slid

black and fizzing to a rung
above eye-level,
knees jack knives,

A high-jumper's, bat mouth
slit grinning
into the fur belly—

helpful: peaches
out there, they keep growing
rounder and rounder

on branches wheeled low
by their weight over
roasted grass blades; sun

and moon, also, evolve
round this mountain
terrace, wrinkling now

with deadly green
emotion: All things
are here, monstrous convulsed

rose (don't anyone
dare come), sounding through
our caves, I hear them.

~~~~~~~~~~~~~~~~~~~~~~~~~~~~~~~~~~~~~

W. D. SNODGRASS

~~~~~~~~~~~~~~~~~~

Looking

What was I looking for today?
All that poking under the rugs,
Peering under the lamps and chairs,
Or going from room to room that way,
Forever up and down the stairs
Like someone stupid with sleep or drugs.

Everywhere I was, was wrong.
I started turning the drawers out, then
I was staring in at the icebox door
Wondering if I'd been there long
Wondering what I was looking for.
Later on, I think I went back again.

Where did the rest of the time go?
Was I down cellar? I can't recall

Finding the light switch, or the last
Place I've had it, or how I'd know
I didn't look at it and go past.
Or whether it's what I want, at all.

Two Girls

I saw again in a dream the other night
Something I saw in daylight years ago,
A path in the rainy woods, a shaft of light,
And two girls walking together through shadow,
Through dazzle, till I lost them on their way
In gloom embowering beyond the glade.
The bright oblivion that belongs to day
Covered their steps, nothing of them remained,

Until the darkness brought them forth again
To the rainy glitter and the silver light,
The ancient leaves that had not fallen then.
Two girls, going forever out of sight,
Talking of lovers, maybe, and of love:
Not that blind life they'd be the mothers of.

HOWARD MOSS

Great Spaces

I would worship if I could
Man, woman, child, or dog,
Strip the desert from my back,
Spill an ocean from each eye,
And like those saints who trust to luck

Sit for years under a tree.
I live now in a dirty city
That prowls the sky and is my shade;
Only a low, uneasy light
Gathers there, a light low-keyed

Amid great spaces and great times.
They soon grow smaller. I forget
What months and years once swam through me
As I walked into their great rooms,
Forgotten rooms, forgotten scenes,

And out in space a statue stands
That will not gloss its meaning. Near
Its pedestal, and on its hands
And knees, a figure, wild, unshorn,
Lifts its head to speak. It says,

"Nothing is unwilling to be born."

The Wars

How can I tell you of the terrible cries
Never sounded, of the nerves that fail,
Not in jungle warfare or a southern jail,
But in some botched affair where two people sit
Quite calmly under a blood-red lamp
In a Chinese restaurant, a ludicrous swamp
Of affection, fear drowning in the amber
Tea when no word comes to mind
To stand for the blood already spilled,
For rejection, denial, for all those years
Of damage done in the polite wars?

And what do I know of the terrible cries
That are really sounded on the real hill
Where the soldiers sweat in the Asian night
And the Asians sweat where the soldiers flail
The murderous grass, and the peasants reel
Back in a rain of gasoline,
And the shells come home and the bombs come down
Quite calmly under a blood-red moon
Not far from China, and the young are killed,
Mere numerals in the casualties
Of this year's war, and the war of years?

He stands with a knife in the Daily News.
They are snaking their way into the hills.
She is walking up Broadway to hurt again.
They are fleeing under a hail of shells.
He is taking her neck into his hands.
A human seed squats in the dark.
She is scalding the baby in the bath.
He feels the bullet enter his skin.
She spits in the face of the riot squad.
They are sitting down, they are opening wounds.

JAMES DICKEY

Deer Among Cattle

Here and there in the searing beam
Of my hand going through the night meadow
They all are grazing

With pins of human light in their eyes.
A wild one also is eating
The human grass,

Slender, graceful, domesticated
By darkness, among the bred-
for-slaughter,

Having bounded their paralyzed fence
And inclined his branched forehead onto
Their green frosted table,

The only live thing in this flashlight
Who can leave whenever he wishes,
Turn grass into forest,

Foreclose inhuman brightness from his eyes
But stands here still, unperturbed,
In their wide-open country,

The sparks from my hand in his pupils
Unmatched anywhere among cattle,

Grazing with them the night of the hammer
As one of their own who shall rise.

LOUIS SIMPSON

Walt Whitman at Bear Mountain

. . . life which does not give the preference to any other life, of
any previous period, which therefore prefers its own existence . . .

—ORTEGA Y GASSET

Neither on horseback nor seated,
But like himself, squarely on two feet,
The poet of death and lilacs
Loafs by the footpath. Even the bronze looks alive
Where it is folded like cloth. And he seems friendly.

"Where is the Mississippi panorama
And the girl who played the piano?
Where are you, Walt?
The Open Road goes to the used-car lot.

"Where is the nation you promised?
These houses built of wood sustain
Colossal snows,
And the light above the street is sick to death.

"As for the people—see how they neglect you!
Only a poet pauses to read the inscription."

"I am here," he answered.
"It seems you have found me out.
Yet, did I not warn you that it was Myself
I advertised? Were my words not sufficiently plain?

"I gave no prescriptions,
And those who have taken my moods for prophecies

Mistake the matter."
Then, vastly amused—"Why do you reproach me?
I freely confess I am wholly disreputable.
Yet I am happy, because you have found me out."

A crocodile in wrinkled metal loafing . . .

Then all the realtors,
Pickpockets, salesmen, and the actors performing
Official scenarios,
Turned a deaf ear, for they had contracted
American dreams.

But the man who keeps a store on a lonely road,
And the housewife who knows she's dumb,
And the earth, are relieved.

All that grave weight of America
Cancelled! Like Greece and Rome.
The future in ruins!
The castles, the prisons, the cathedrals
Unbuilding, and roses
Blossoming from the stones that are not there . . .

The clouds are lifting from the high Sierras,
The Bay mists clearing.
And the angel in the gate, the flowering plum,
Dances like Italy, imagining red.

Outward

The staff slips from the hand
Hissing and swims on the polished floor.
It glides away to the desert.

It floats like a bird or lily
On the waves, to the ones who are arriving.
And if no god arrives,

Then everything yearns outward.
The honeycomb cell brims over
And the atom is broken in light.

Machines have made their god. They walk or fly.
The towers bend like Magi, mountains weep,
Needles go mad, and metal sheds a tear.

*

The astronaut is lifted
Away from the world, and drifts.
How easy it is to be there!

How easy to be anyone, anything but oneself!
The metal of the plane is breathing;
Sinuously it swims through the stars.

ANTHONY HECHT

Improvisations on Aesop

It was a tortoise aspiring to fly
That murdered Aeschylus. All men must die.

The crocodile rends man and beast to death
And has St. Francis' birds to pick his teeth.

Lorenzo sponsored artists, and the ant
Must save to give the grasshopper a grant.

The blind man bears the lame, who gives him eyes;
Only the weak make common enterprise.

Frogs into bulls, sows' ears into silk purses,
These are our hopes in youth, in age our curses.

Spare not the rod, lest thy child be undone,
And at the gallows cry, "Behold thy son."

The Fox and Buddha put away their lust:
"Sour grapes!" they cry. "All but the soul is dust!"

An ass may look at an angel, Balaam was shown;
Cudgel thy wits, and leave thine ass alone.

Is not that pastoral instruction sweet
Which says who shall be eaten, who shall eat?

Pig

In the manger of course were cows and the Child Himself
                    Was like unto a lamb
Who should come in the fulness of time on an ass's back
                    Into Jerusalem

And all things be redeemed—the suckling babe
                    Lie safe in the serpent's home
And the lion eat straw like the ox and roar its love
                    to Mark and to Jerome

And God's Peaceable Kingdom return among them all
                    Save one full of offense
Into which the thousand fiends of a human soul
                    Were cast and driven hence

And the one thus cured gone up into the hills
                    To worship and to pray:
O Swine that takest away our sins
                    That takest away

Giant Tortoise

I am related to stones
The slow accretion of moss where dirt is wedged
Long waxy hair that can split boulders.
Events are not important.

I live in my bone
Recalling the hour of my death.
It takes more toughness than most have got.
Or a saintliness.

Strength of a certain kind, anyway.
Bald toothless clumsy perhaps
With all the indignity of old age
But age is not important.

There is nothing worth remembering
But the silver glint in the muck
The thickening of great trees
The hard crust getting harder.

JAMES   MERRILL

Lorelei

The stones of kin and friend
Stretch off into a trembling, sweatlike haze.

They may not after all be stepping-stones
But you have followed them. Each strands you, then

Does not. Not yet. Not here.
Is it a crossing? Is there no way back?

Soft gleams lap the base of the one behind you
On which a black girl sings and combs her hair.

It's she who some day (when your stone is in place)
Will see that much further into the golden vagueness

Forever about to clear. Love with his chisel
Deepens the lines begun upon your face.

Part of the Vigil

... shrinking to enter, did. Your heart
Was large—you'd often told me—large but light,
Ant palace, tubercular coral sponge amazed
With passages, quite weightless in your breast.
(Or did my entrance weigh? You never said.)
In sunlit outer galleries I pondered
Names, dates, political slogans, lyrics,
Football scores, obscenities too, scrawled
Everywhere dense as lace. How alike we were!
More than pleased, I penetrated further.
Strung haphazard now through the red gloom
Were little, doorless, crudely lighted chambers:
Four waxen giants at supper; the late king;
A dust-furred dog; a whore mottled with cold,
Legs in air; your motorbike; a friend,
Glass raised despite the bandage round his head,
His eyes' false shine. What had happened to them all?
Yet other cells appeared empty but lit,
Or darkly, unimaginably tenanted.
From one, a word sobbed over, "Waste ... the waste ..."
Where was the terrace, the transparency
So striking far away? In my fall I struck
An iron surface (so! your heart was heavy)
Hot through clothing. Snatched myself erect.

Beneath, great valves were gasping, wheezing. What
If all you knew of me were down there, leaking
Fluids at once abubble, pierced by fierce
Impulsions of unfeeling, life, limb turning
To burning cubes, to devil's dice, to ash—
What if my effigy were down there? What,
Dear god, if it were not!
If it were nowhere in your heart!
Here I turned back. Of the rest I do not speak.
Nor was your heart so cleverly constructed
I needed more than time to get outside—
Time, scorned as I scorned the waiting daylight.
Before resuming my true size, there came
A place in which one could have scratched one's name.
But what rights had I? Didn't your image,
Still unharmed, deep in my own saved skin
Blaze on? You might yet see it, see by it.
Nothing else mattered.

Remora

This life is deep and dense
Beyond all seeing, yet one sees, in spite
Of being littler, a degree or two
Further than those one is attracted to.

Pea-brained, myopic, often brutal,
When chosen they have no defense—
A sucking sore there on the belly's pewter—
And where two go could be one's finer sense.

Who now descends from a machine
Plumed with bubbles, death in his right hand?
Lunge, numbskull! One, two, three worlds boil.
Thanks for the lift. There are other fish in the sea.

Still on occasion as by oversight
One lets be taken clinging fast
In heavenly sunshine to the corpse a slight
Tormented self, live, dapper, black-and-white.

GALWAY KINNELL

In the Hotel of Lost Light

1

In the left-
hand sag the drunk smelling of autopsies
died in, my body slumped out
into the shape of his, I watch, as he
must have watched, a fly
tangled in mouth-glue, whining his wings,
concentrated wholly on
time, time, losing his way worse
down the downward-winding stairs, his wings
whining for life as he shrivels
in the gaze
from the spider's clasped forebrains, the abstracted stare
in which even the nightmare spatters out its horrors
and dies.

Now the fly
ceases to struggle, his wings
flutter out the music blooming with failure
of one who gets ready to die, as Roland's horn, winding down
from the Pyrenees, saved its dark, full flourishes
for last.

2

In the light
left behind by the little
spiders of blood who garbled
their memoirs across his shoulders
and chest, the room
echoes with the tiny thrumps
of crotch hairs plucking themselves
from their spots, on the stripped skin
the love-sick crab lice
struggle to unstick themselves and sprint from the doomed
    position—

and stop,
heads buried
for one last taste of the love-flesh.

3

Flesh
of his excavated flesh,
fill of his emptiness,
after-amanuensis of his after-life,
I write out
for him in this languished alphabet
of worms, these last words
of himself, post for him
his final postcards to posterity.

4

"I sat out by twigfires flaring in grease strewn from the
    pimpled limbs of hen,
I blacked out into oblivion by that crack in the curb where
    the forget-me blooms,
I saw the ferris wheel writing its huge, desolate zeroes in neon
    on the evening skies,

I painted my footsoles purple for the day when the beautiful
    color would show,
I staggered death-sentences down empty streets, the cobble-
    stones assured me, *it shall be so,*
I heard my own cries already howled inside bottles the waves
    washed up on beaches,
I ghostwrote my prayers myself in the body-Arabic of these
    nightmares.

"If the deskman knocks, griping again
about the sweet, excremental
odor of opened cadaver creeping out
from under the door, tell him, 'Friend, *To Live*
has a poor cousin,
who calls tonight, who pronounces the family name
To Leave, she
changes each visit the flesh-rags on her bones.' "

5

Violet bruises come out
all over his flesh, as invisible
fists start beating him a last time; the whine
of omphalos blood starts up again, the puffed
bellybutton explodes, the carnal
nightmare soars back to the beginning.

6

As for the bones to be tossed
into the aceldama back of the potting shop, among
shards and lumps
which caught vertigo and sagged away
into mud, or crawled out of fire
crazed or exploded, they shall re-arise
in the pear tree, in spring, to shine down
on two clasping what they dream is one another.

As for these words scattered into the future—
posterity

is one invented too deep in its past
to hear them.

7

The foregoing scribed down
in March, of the year Seventy,
on my sixteen-thousandth night of war and madness,
in the Hotel of Lost Light, under the freeway
which roams out into the dark
of the moon, in the absolute spell
of departure, and by the light
from the joined hemispheres of the spider's eyes.

ALAN DUGAN

Elegy

I know but will not tell
you, Aunt Irene, why there
are soapsuds in the whiskey:
Uncle Robert had to have
a drink while shaving. May
there be no bloodshed in your house
this morning of my father's death
and no unkept appearance
in the living, since he has
to wear the rouge and lipstick
of your ceremony, mother,
for the first and last time:
father, hello and goodbye.

The Attempted Rescue

I came out on the wrong
side of time and saw
the rescue party leave.
"How long must we wait?"
I said. "Forever. You
are too far gone to save,
too dangerous to carry off
the precipice, and frozen stiff
besides. So long. You
can have our brandy. That's life."

For Masturbation

I have allowed myself
this corner and am God.
Here in the must
beneath their stoop
I will do as I will,
either as act as act,
or dream for the sake of dreams,
and if they find me out
in rocket ships or jets
working to get away,

then let my left great-toe-
nail grow into the inside knob
of my right ankle bone and let
my fingernails make eight new moons
temporarily in the cold salt marches of my palms!
THIS IS THE WAY IT IS, and if
it is "a terrible disgrace"
it is as I must will,
because I am not them
though I am theirs to kill.

A Sawyer's Rage Against
Trees Noble as Horses

1.

Inwardly centered like a child
sucking soda through a straw,
they have their noses in the dirt,
greedily absent, blinded, while
their green behinds in the wind
wave back and forth. Oh I can
hit them and they won't hit back.
Oh let them all come down, slowly at the first inclination from
the vertical, then faster, then
crashing in passion! There is
a hallelujah from the dust and birds,
and insects are set free of hell
in devilish shapes to shrivel in
the solid glare of the day, fools
to the contrary, who maintain
that Christ is down from the heights
by this, to the mother earth again.

2.

It is even, the way the trees,
in coming up from the ground,
from nothing, from a nut,
take liberties in spreading out
like animals, like us. But, brutes
of a chosen ground, they stand
around in suction, dark, grouped
like witnesses afraid to act
beside the accidents of roads
and more afraid to cross except
packed in a squirrel's cheek,
in nuts, or in a fairy's flight

of seed. Their undersides are dark
in contrast to the strong, blond,
human inner arm; even the ground
beneath them is a hairy damp,
dirty as groins. Oh we will cut
them down to boards, pulp, dust,
and size: fury the ax, fury the saw
will cure their spreading stands;
courage will make the world plain.

Poem

A man with a box walked up to a woman with a boy, gave
    the box
to the boy, said, "Don't drop it for a change," and kissed
the woman, suckling up her rosebud from her mud-color.
    It bloomed.
He said, "Let's go." They went, with technicolor haloes of
    the usual
around them. Why? Because: They come from a star, live by
    its light,
and burn with it here in the dark outside of the department
    store.

On Hat: On Vertical Mobility
as a Concept

From the official hurry on the top floor
and through the irony on the working floors
down to the sleep stolen in the basement,
the company went on incorporate and firm,
drumming like an engine through the spring day.
Standing still but often going up and down
while breaking in a new winter felt hat,
the elevator operator was the best man in

the place in humor. Going from the thieves
at the top to the bums in the cellar
and past the tame working people in between,
he was denoting Plato's ideal form of Hat
vertically in an unjust state in the spring:
he did nothing but social service for nothing
as a form to be walked on like stairs.

ALVIN FEINMAN

Pilgrim Heights

Something, something, the heart here
Misses, something it knows it needs
Unable to bless—the wind passes;
A swifter shadow sweeps the reeds,
The heart a colder contrast brushes.

So this fool, face-forward, belly
Pressed among the rushes, plays out
His pulse to the dune's long slant
Down from blue to bluer element,
The bold encompassing drink of air

And namelessness, a length compound
Of want and oneness the shore's mumbling
Distantly tells—something a wing's
Dry pivot stresses, carved
Through barrens of stillness and glare:

The naked close of light in light,
Light's spare embrace of blade and tremor
Stealing the generous eye's plunder

Like a breathing banished from the lung's
Fever, lost in parenthetic air.

Raiding these nude recesses, the hawk
Resumes his yielding balance, his shadow
Swims the field, the sands beyond,
The narrow edges fed out to light,
To the sea's eternal licking monochrome.

The foolish hip, the elbow bruise
Upright from the dampening mat,
The twisted grasses turn, unthatch,
Light-headed blood renews its stammer—
Apart, below, the dazed eye catches

A darkened figure abruptly measured
Where folding breakers lay their whites;
The heart from its height starts downward,
Swum in that perfect pleasure
It knows it needs, unable to bless.

Scene Recalled

How should I not have preferred
The flinted salt of occasion?

The stern
Adequation I required of my eye:

    A time
    Of gulls riding out,
    Of the tide going cold at my ankles;

    A scene
    Held tall as postponement,
    As authority printed to landscape.

You are not the first man who exacted
Of flight it ascend through his shoulder;

Through the copper of nightfall the silver.

Noon

And something not themselves, a thing
That lags, or overbends, a white
That waits in tightly knuckled things . . .

The buildings hold their height,
The air itself its care
For clarity, for outline, for the flight
Of birds
      —as though an emptiness
Could fall, or fill all space
With some forgottenness: that thing
Out of which nothing knows itself . . .

In every gesture of the face, the hand,
What loss or trust is mastering its ground?

Great Stroke of Noon that does not sound.

True Night

So it is midnight, and all
The angels of ordinary day gone,
The abiding absence between day and day
Comes like true and only rain
Comes instant, eternal, again:

As though an air had opened without sound
In which all things are sanctified,
In which they are at prayer—

The drunken man in his stupor,
The madman's lucid shrinking circle;

As though all things shone perfectly,
Perfected in self-discrepancy:
The widow wedded to her grief,
The hangman haloed in remorse—
I should not rearrange a leaf,

No more than wish to lighten stones
Or still the sea where it still roars—
Here every grief requires its grief,
Here every longing thing is lit
Like darkness at an altar.

As long as truest night is long,
Let no discordant wing
Corrupt these sorrows into song.

W. S. MERWIN

The Lake

Did you exist
ever

our clouds separated while it was still dark
then I could not sleep the sleep of a child
I got up to look for you
bringing my silence
all of it

no father in the house at least

I got my boat
that we had saved for each other
a white creature my
wise elder
You rustled as it slid
from shore

I lay there
looking down while the mist was torn
looking down
where
was the Indian village
said to be drowned there

one glimpse and I would have hung
fixed in its sky
when the dawn was gone
and the morning star
and the wind
and the sun
and the calling around you

Man with One Leaf
in October Night

The leaves turn black when they have learned how to
so does the day
but in the wind of the first hours of darkness
sudden joy sent
from an unknown tree
I have not deserved you

Early January

A year has come to us as though out of hiding
It has arrived from an unknown distance

From beyond the visions of the old
Everyone waited for it by the wrong roads
And it is hard for us now to be sure it is here
A stranger to nothing
In our hiding places

The Thread

Unrolling the black thread
through the tunnel
you come to the wide wall
of shoes
the soles standing
out in the air you breathe
crowded from side to side
floor to ceiling
and no names
and no door
and the bodies
stacked before them like bottles
generation upon
generation
upon generation
with their threads
asleep in their hands
and the tunnel is full
of their bodies
from there
all the way to the end of the mountain
the beginning of time
the light of day
the bird
and you are unrolling
the Sibyl's song
that is trying to reach her
beyond your dead

The Web

So it's mine
this leg of a thin gray travelling animal
caught in the web again
tearing
in the stocking of blood

the old scars waking opening
in the form of a web

the seamless fabric itself bleeding
where it clings

and all this time dark wings
cries
cries flying over at a great height

o web

over the sand you are woven
over the water you are woven
over the snow you are woven
over the grass you are woven
over the mountains you are woven
over the heads of the lambs you are woven
over the fish you are woven
over the faces you are woven
over the clouds you are woven
over pain itself you are woven

the tears glint on you like dew
the blood is spreading wherever you have held me
the days and the nights
keep their distance
without a sound

but I remember also the ringing spaces
when I have crossed you like a hand on a harp
and even now
in the echoless sky the birds pursue our music

hoping to hear it again

ROBERT BLY

Looking into a Face

Conversation brings us so close! Opening
The surfs of the body,
Bringing fish up near the sun,
And stiffening the backbones of the sea!

I have wandered in a face, for hours,
Passing through dark fires.
I have risen to a body
Not yet born,
Existing like a light around the body,
Through which the body moves like a sliding moon.

Waking from Sleep

Inside the veins there are navies setting forth,
Tiny explosions at the water lines.
And seagulls weaving in the wind of the salty blood.

It is the morning. The country has slept the whole winter.
Window seats were covered with fur skins, the yard was full
Of stiff dogs, and hands that clumsily held heavy books.

Now we wake, and rise from bed, and eat breakfast!—
Shouts rise from the harbor of the blood,
Mist, and masts rising, the knock of wooden tackle in the
    sunlight.

Now we sing, and do tiny dances on the kitchen floor.
Our whole body is like a harbor at dawn;
We know that our master has left us for the day.

Snowfall in the Afternoon

I

The grass is half covered with snow.
It was the sort of snowfall that starts in late afternoon,
And now the little houses of the grass are growing dark.

II

If I reached my hands down, near the earth,
I could take handfuls of darkness!
A darkness was always there, which we never noticed.

III

As the snow grows heavier, the cornstalks fade farther away,
And the barn moves nearer to the house.
The barn moves all alone in the growing storm.

IV

The barn is full of corn, and moving toward us now,
Like a hulk blown toward us in a storm at sea;
All the sailors on deck have been blind for many years.

Afternoon Sleep

I

I was descending from the mountains of sleep.
Asleep I had gazed east over a sunny field,
And sat on the running board of an old Model A.
I awoke happy, for I had dreamt of my wife,
And the loneliness hiding in grass and weeds
That lies near a man over thirty, and suddenly enters.

II

When Joe Sjolie grew tired, he sold his farm,
Even his bachelor rocker, and did not come back.
He left his dog behind in the cob shed.
The dog refused to take food from strangers.

III

I drove out to that farm when I awoke;
Alone on a hill, sheltered by trees.
The matted grass lay around the house.
When I climbed the porch, the door was open.
Inside were old abandoned books,
And instructions to Norwegian immigrants.

SAMUEL MENASHE

Voyage

Water opens without end
At the bow of a ship
Rising to descend
Away from it

Days become one
I am who I was

*

Sleep

gives wood its grain
dreams knot the wood

*

The apple of my eye

now goes to seed
Wrinkles undermine
a dwindling cheek
No kiss ekes out
the stemmed mouth

Only the nose
does not shrink

*

Sudden Shadow

Crow I scorn you
Caw everywhere
You'll not subdue
This blue air

*

Reeds rise from water

rippling under my eyes
Bullrushes tuft the shore

At every instant I expect
what is hidden everywhere

*

Promised Land

At the edge
Of a world
Beyond my eyes
Beautiful
I know Exile
Is always
Green with hope—
The river
We cannot cross
Flows forever

*

Sunset, Central Park

A wall of windows
Ignited by the sun
Burns in one column
Of fire on the lake
Night follows day
As embers break

JAMES WRIGHT

Lying in a Hammock at William Duffy's Farm in Pine Island, Minnesota

Over my head, I see the bronze butterfly,
Asleep on the black trunk,
Blowing like a leaf in green shadow.
Down the ravine behind the empty house,
The cowbells follow one another
Into the distances of the afternoon.
To my right,
In a field of sunlight between two pines,
The droppings of last year's horses
Blaze up into golden stones.
I lean back, as the evening darkens and comes on.
A chicken hawk floats over, looking for home.
I have wasted my life.

Youth

Strange bird,
His song remains secret.
He worked too hard to read books.
He never heard how Sherwood Anderson
Got out of it, and fled to Chicago, furious to free himself
From his hatred of factories.
My father toiled fifty years
At Hazel-Atlas Glass,
Caught among girders that smash the kneecaps
Of dumb honyaks.
Did he shudder with hatred in the cold shadow of grease?
Maybe. But my brother and I do know
He came home as quiet as the evening.

He will be getting dark, soon,
And loom through new snow.
I know his ghost will drift home
To the Ohio River, and sit down, alone,
Whittling a root.
He will say nothing.
The waters flow past, older, younger
Than he is, or I am.

To the Muse

It is all right. All they do
Is go in by dividing
One rib from another. I wouldn't
Lie to you. It hurts
Like nothing I know. All they do
Is burn their way in with a wire.
It forks in and out a little like the tongue
Of that frightened garter snake we caught
At Cloverfield, you and me, Jenny
So long ago.

I would lie to you
If I could.
But the only way I can get you to come up
Out of the suckhole, the south face
Of the Powhatan pit, is to tell you
What you know:

You come up after dark, you poise alone
With me on the shore.
I lead you back to this world.

Three lady doctors in Wheeling open
Their offices at night.
I don't have to call them, they are always there.
But they only have to put the knife once
Under your breast.
Then they hang their contraption.
And you bear it.

It's awkward a while. Still, it lets you
Walk about on tiptoe if you don't
Jiggle the needle.
It might stab your heart, you see.
The blade hangs in your lung and the tube
Keeps it draining.
That way they only have to stab you
Once. Oh Jenny,
I wish to God I had made this world, this scurvy
And disastrous place. I
Didn't, I can't bear it
Either, I don't blame you, sleeping down there
Face down in the unbelievable silk of spring,
Muse of black sand,
Alone.

I don't blame you, I know
The place where you lie.
I admit everything. But look at me.

How can I live without you?
Come up to me, love,
Out of the river, or I will
Come down to you.

A. R. AMMONS

Early Morning
in Early April

The mist rain this morning made glass,
a glittery preponderance, hung baubles
spangled to birch-twig jewelry,

and made the lawn support, item by
item, the air's weight, a lesson as a
various instruction with a theme: and

how odd, the maple branches underlaced
with glaring beadwork: what to make of it:
what to make of a mist whose characteristic

is a fine manyness coming dull in a wide
oneness: what to make of the glass
erasures, glass: the yew's partly lost.

The City Limits

When you consider the radiance, that it does not withhold
itself but pours its abundance without selection into every
nook and cranny not overhung or hidden; when you consider

that birds' bones make no awful noise against the light but
lie low in the light as in a high testimony; when you consider
the radiance, that it will look into the guiltiest

swervings of the weaving heart and bear itself upon them,
not flinching into disguise or darkening; when you consider
the abundance of such resource as illuminates the glow-blue

bodies and gold-skeined wings of flies swarming the dumped
guts of a natural slaughter or the coil of shit and in no
way winces from its storms of generosity; when you consider

that air or vacuum, snow or shale, squid or wolf, rose or lichen,
each is accepted into as much light as it will take, then
the heart moves roomier, the man stands and looks about, the

leaf does not increase itself above the grass, and the dark
work of the deepest cells is of a tune with May bushes
and fear lit by the breadth of such calmly turns to praise.

Circles

I can't decide whether
the backyard stuff's
central or irrelevant:
how matted rank the mint is! and
some of the iris stalks are so
crooked rich
the blossoms can't burst
(scant weeds
pop their flowers fast) loose
and the pansies keep
jointing up another blooming tier:
I can't figure out what
the whole green wish again
is, tips pushing hard into
doing the same, last

year again, the year before:
something nearer than
the pleasure of
circles drives into the next
moment and the next.

TED HUGHES

Crow's Nerve Fails

Crow, feeling his brain slip,
Finds his every feather the fossil of a murder.

Who murdered all these?
These living dead, that root in his nerves and his blood
Till he is visibly black?

How can he fly from his feathers?
And why have they homed on him?

Is he the archive of their accusations?
Or their ghostly purpose, their pining vengeance?
Or their unforgiven prisoner?

He cannot be forgiven.

His prison is the earth. Clothed in his conviction,
Trying to remember his crimes

Heavily he flies.

Crow's Fall

When Crow was white he decided the sun was too white.
He decided it glared much too whitely.
He decided to attack it and defeat it.

He got his strength flush and in full glitter.
He clawed and fluffed his rage up.
He aimed his beak direct at the sun's centre.

He laughed himself to the centre of himself

And attacked.

At his battle cry trees grew suddenly old,
Shadows flattened.

But the sun brightened—
It brightened, and Crow returned charred black.

He opened his mouth but what came out was charred black.

"Up there," he managed,
"Where white is black and black is white, I won."

A Childish Prank

Man's and woman's bodies lay without souls,
Dully gaping, foolishly staring, inert
On the flowers of Eden.
God pondered.

The problem was so great, it dragged him asleep.

Crow laughed.
He bit the Worm, God's only son,
Into two writhing halves.

He stuffed into man the tail half
With the wounded end hanging out.

He stuffed the head half headfirst into woman
And it crept in deeper and up
To peer out through her eyes
Calling its tail-half to join up quickly, quickly
Because O it was painful.

Man awoke being dragged across the grass.
Woman awoke to see him coming.
Neither knew what had happened.

God went on sleeping.

Crow went on laughing.

Fragment of an Ancient Tablet

Above—the well-known lips, delicately downed.
Below—beard between thighs.

Above—her brow, the notable casket of gems.
Below—the belly with its blood-knot.

Above—many a painful frown.
Below—the ticking bomb of the future.

Above—her perfect teeth, with the hint of a fang at the
    corner.
Below—the millstones of two worlds.

Above—a word and a sigh.
Below—gouts of blood and babies.

Above—the face, shaped like a perfect heart.
Below—the heart's torn face.

Glimpse

"O leaves," Crow sang, trembling, "O leaves—"

The touch of a leaf's edge at his throat
Guillotined further comment.

                    Nevertheless
Speechless he continued to stare at the leaves
Through the god's head instantly substituted.

❦

FRANK O'HARA

To the Harbormaster

I wanted to be sure to reach you;
though my ship was on the way it got caught
in some moorings. I am always tying up
and then deciding to depart. In storms and
at sunset, with the metallic coils of the tide
around my fathomless arms, I am unable
to understand the forms of my vanity
or I am hard alee with my Polish rudder
in my hand and the sun sinking. To
you I offer my hull and the tattered cordage
of my will. The terrible channels where
the wind drives me against the brown lips
of the reeds are not all behind me. Yet
I trust the sanity of my vessel; and
if it sinks, it may well be in answer
to the reasoning of the eternal voices,
the waves which have kept me from reaching you.

Poem

The eager note on my door said "Call me,
call when you get in!" so I quickly threw
a few tangerines into my overnight bag,
straightened my eyelids and shoulders, and

headed straight for the door. It was autumn
by the time I got around the corner, oh all
unwilling to be either pertinent or bemused, but
the leaves were brighter than grass on the sidewalk!

Funny, I thought, that the lights are on this late
and the hall door open; still up at this hour, a
champion jai-alai player like himself? Oh fie!
for shame! What a host, so zealous! And he was

there in the hall, flat on a sheet of blood that
ran down the stairs. I did appreciate it. There are few
hosts who so thoroughly prepare to greet a guest
only casually invited, and that several months ago.

The Hunter

He set out and kept hunting
and hunting. Where, he thought
and thought, is the real chamois?
and can I kill it where it is?
He had brought with him only a dish
of pears. The autumn wind soared
above the trails where the drops
of the chamois led him further.
The leaves dropped around him
like pie-plates. The stars fell
one by one into his eyes and burnt.

There is a geography which holds
its hands just so far from the breast
and pushes you away, crying so.
He went on to strange hills where
the stones were still warm from feet,
and then on and on. There were clouds
at his knees, his eyelashes
had grown thick from the colds,
as the fur of the bear does
in winter. Perhaps, he thought, I am
asleep, but he did not freeze to death.

There were little green needles
everywhere. And then manna fell.
He knew, above all, that he was now
approved, and his strength increased.
He saw the world below him, brilliant
as a floor, and steaming with gold,
with distance. There were occasionally
rifts in the cloud where the face
of a woman appeared, frowning. He
had gone higher. He wore ermine.
He thought, why did I come? and then,
I have come to rule! The chamois came.

The chamois found him and they came
in droves to humiliate him. Alone,
in the clouds, he was humiliated.

Chez Jane

The white chocolate jar full of petals
swills odds and ends around in a dizzying eye
of four o'clocks now and to come. The tiger,
marvellously striped and irritable, leaps
on the table and without disturbing a hair

of the flowers' breathless attention, pisses
into the pot, right down its delicate spout.
A whisper of steam goes up from that porcelain
eurythra. "Saint-Saëns!" it seems to be whispering,
curling unerringly around the furry nuts
of the terrible puss, who is mentally flexing.
Ah be with me always, spirit of noisy
contemplation in the studio, the Garden
of Zoos, the eternally fixed afternoons!
There, while music scratches its scrofulous
stomach, the brute beast emerges and stands,
clear and careful, knowing always the exact peril
at this moment caressing his fangs with
a tongue given wholly to luxurious usages;
which only a moment before dropped aspirin
in this sunset of roses, and now throws a chair
in the air to aggravate the truly menacing.

River

Whole days would go by, and later their years,
while I thought of nothing but its darkness
drifting like a bridge against the sky.
Day after day I dreamily sought its melancholy,
its searchings, its soft banks enfolded me,
and upon my lengthening neck its kiss
was murmuring like a wound. My very life
became the inhalation of its weedy ponderings
and sometimes in the sunlight my eyes,
walled in water, would glimpse the pathway
to the great sea. For it was there I was being borne.
Then for a moment my strengthening arms
would cry out upon the leafy crest of the air
like whitecaps, and lightning, swift as pain,
would go through me on its way to the forest,
and I'd sink back upon that brutal tenderness

that bore me on, that held me like a slave
in its liquid distances of eyes, and one day,
though weeping for my caresses, would abandon me,
moment of infinitely salty air! sun fluttering
like a signal! upon the open flesh of the world.

JOHN ASHBERY

Song

The song tells us of our old way of living,
Of life in former times. Fragrance of florals,
How things merely ended when they ended,
Of beginning again into a sigh. Later

Some movement is reversed and the urgent masks
Speed toward a totally unexpected end
Like clocks out of control. Is this the gesture
That was meant, long ago, the curving in

Of frustrated denials, like jungle foliage
And the simplicity of the ending all to be let go
In quick, suffocating sweetness? The day
Puts toward a nothingness of sky

Its face of rusticated brick. Sooner or later,
The cars lament, the whole business will be hurled down.
Meanwhile we sit, scarcely daring to speak,
To breathe, as though this closeness cost us life.

The pretensions of a past will some day
Make it over into progress, a growing up,

As beautiful as a new history book
With uncut pages, unseen illustrations,

And the purpose of the many stops and starts will be made
    clear:
Backing into the old affair of not wanting to grow
Into the night, which becomes a house, a parting of the ways
Taking us far into sleep. A dumb love.

A Blessing in Disguise

Yes, they are alive and can have those colors,
But I, in my soul, am alive too.
I feel I must sing and dance, to tell
Of this in a way, that knowing you may be drawn to me.

And I sing amid despair and isolation
Of the chance to know you, to sing of me
Which are you. You see,
You hold me up to the light in a way

I should never have expected, or suspected, perhaps
Because you always tell me I am you,
And right. The great spruces loom.
I am yours to die with, to desire.

I cannot ever think of me, I desire you
For a room in which the chairs ever
Have their backs turned to the light
Inflicted on the stone and paths, the real trees

That seem to shine at me through a lattice toward you.
If the wild light of this January day is true
I pledge me to be truthful unto you
Whom I cannot ever stop remembering.

Remembering to forgive. Remember to pass beyond you into
    the day

On the wings of the secret you will never know.
Taking me from myself, in the path
Which the pastel girth of the day has assigned to me.

I prefer "you" in the plural, I want "you."
You must come to me, all golden and pale
Like the dew and the air.
And then I start getting this feeling of exaltation.

JAMES SCHUYLER

February

A chimney, breathing a little smoke.
The sun, I can't see
making a bit of pink
I can't quite see in the blue.
The pink of five tulips
at five P.M. on the day before March first.
The green of the tulip stems and leaves
like something I can't remember,
finding a jack-in-the-pulpit
a long time ago and far away.
Why it was December then
and the sun was on the sea
by the temples we'd gone to see.
One green wave moved in the violet sea
like the UN Building on big evenings,
green and wet
while the sky turns violet.
A few almond trees
had a few flowers, like a few snowflakes
out of the blue looking pink in the light.

A gray hush
in which the boxy trucks roll up Second Avenue
into the sky. They're just
going over the hill.
The green leaves of the tulips on my desk
like grass light on flesh,
and a green-copper steeple
and streaks of cloud beginning to glow.
I can't get over
how it all works in together
like a woman who just came to her window
and stands there filling it
jogging her baby in her arms.
She's so far off. Is it the light
that makes the baby pink?
I can see the little fists
and the rocking-horse motion of her breasts.
It's getting grayer and gold and chilly.
Two dog-size lions face each other
at the corners of a roof.
It's the yellow dust inside the tulips.
It's the shape of a tulip.
It's the water in the drinking glass the tulips are in.
It's a day like any other.

The Master of the Golden Glow

An irregular rattle (shutters) and
a ferule tapped
on a blackboard—or where you come from
do they say chalkboard?—anyway it's not any sort of pointer
it's a sash facing west
wood and glass drummed on by autumn tatters.
Say, who are you
anyway? "I think we may have met before.
God knows I've heard enough about you."
That largest maple—
half its leaves an undreamt of butter:

if only safflower oil
were the color of its name
the way olive oil is. "Why,
don't you *like* butter?"
The doctor's youngest son
paddles the canoe while he (the doctor) casts
for mud-flavored carp in the long brackish pond:
Agawam, meaning lake. Lake Pond,
Pond Lake, Lake Lake, Pond Pond,
its short waves jumping up and down
in one place with surplus energy to spend.
Somewhere, out of the wind,
the wind collects a ripe debris.
"I'll tell you who I am: someone
you never met
though on a train you studied a boil on my neck
or bumped into me
leaving a late late party
                    'Sorry'
or saw throwing bones in the ocean
for an inexhaustible retriever."
The wind drops. The sky darkens
to an unfathomable gray
and through hardware cloth one
leaf is seen to fall
describing the helixes of conch-shell cores
gathered in summer, thrown out in autumn.
More litter, less clutter.

An Almanac

Shops take down their awnings;
women go south;
few street lamp leaners;
children run with leaves running at their backs.
In cedar chests sheers and seersuckers displace flannels and
    wools.

Sere leaves of the Scotch marigolds;
crystals of earth melt;
the thorn apple shows its thorns;
a dog tracks the kitchen porch;
wino-hobos attempt surrender to warm asylums.

Caged mink claw;
gulls become pigeons;
snow bends the snow fence.
Heavy food;
rumbling snowplows.

Seats in the examination hall are staggered.
The stars gleam like ice;
a fragment of bone;
in the woods matted leaves;
a yellowish shoot.
A lost key is found;
storm windows are stacked on the beams of the garage.

❧

KENNETH KOCH

We Sailed the Indian Ocean
for a Dime

We sailed the Indian Ocean for a dime
And went into Africa for a penny
Refreshing Argentina
Rewarded us with many silver cars
For our toy train   We went to Kansas City
In the hope of finding quarters there
But instead we sailed the Manila Sea

Old sea pencils without landing quarters
Five dollars drew us to Tangiers
We had saved up enough dimes to purchase the bill
There it lies all crisp and green and light
Take it pick it up in your hands it is mine

We spent the five dollars in Biarritz in seven minutes
But at least we had a good meal and now we set sail
I've heard that Milwaukee is full of dimes and quarters
And that Cincinnati is the place for half dollars
I can see all that silver I can see it and I think I want it
Can see the sunlight lighting those silver faces
In far-off Cincinnati
The slim half dollars lying in the leaves
In the blue autumn weather behind the Conservatory of Music
Oh give me the money
That I may ascend into the sky
For I have been on so many boats and trains
While endlessly seeking the summits of my life!

You Were Wearing

You were wearing your Edgar Allan Poe printed cotton
     blouse.
In each divided up square of the blouse was a picture of Edgar
     Allan Poe.
Your hair was blonde and you were cute. You asked me, "Do
     most boys think that most girls are bad?"
I smelled the mould of your seaside resort hotel bedroom on
     your hair held in place by a John Greenleaf Whittier clip.
"No," I said, "it's girls who think that boys are bad." Then we
     read Snowbound together
And ran around in an attic, so that a little of the blue enamel
     was scraped off my George Washington, Father of His
     Country, shoes.

Mother was walking in the living room, her Strauss Waltzes
     comb in her hair.

We waited for a time and then joined her, only to be served
    tea in cups painted with pictures of Herman Melville
As well as with illustrations from his book *Moby Dick* and
    from his novella, *Benito Cereno.*
Father came in wearing his Dick Tracy necktie: "How about
    a drink, everyone?"
I said, "Let's go outside a while." Then we went onto the
    porch and sat on the Abraham Lincoln swing.
You sat on the eyes, mouth, and beard part, and I sat on the
    knees.
In the yard across the street we saw a snowman holding a
    garbage can lid smashed into a likeness of the mad
    English king, George the Third.

JOSEPH CERAVOLO

The Wind Is Blowing West

1

I am trying to decide to go swimming,
But the sea looks so calm.
All the other boys have gone in.
I can't decide what to do.

I've been waiting in my tent
Expecting to go in.
Have you forgotten to come down?
Can I escape going in?
I was just coming

I was just going in
But lost my pail

2

A boisterous tide is coming up;
I was just looking at it.
The pail is near me
again. My shoulders have sand on them.

Round the edge of the tide
Is the shore. The shore
Is filled with waves.
They are tin waves.

Boisterous tide coming up.
The tide is getting less.

3

Daytime is not a brain,
Living is not a cricket's song.
Why does light diffuse
As earth turns away from the sun?

I want to give my food
To a stranger. I want
to be taken.
What kind of a face do

I have while leaving?
I'm thinking of my friend.

4

I am trying to go swimming
But the sea looks so calm
All boys are gone
I can't decide what to do

I've been waiting to go
Have you come down?
Can I escape

I am just coming
       Just going in

CHARLES OLSON

The Songs of Maximus

SONG 1

      colored pictures
of all things to eat: dirty
postcards
      And words, words, words
all over everything
          No eyes or ears left
to do their own doings (all

invaded, appropriated, outraged, all senses

including the mind, that worker on what is

          And that other sense
made to give even the most wretched, or any of us, wretched,
that consolation (greased
        lulled
even the street-cars

song

SONG 2

　　all
wrong
　　　　And I am asked—ask myself (I, too, covered
with the gurry of it) where
shall we go from here, what can we do
when even the public conveyances
sing?
　　　　how can we go anywhere,
even cross town
　　　　　　　　how get out of anywhere (the bodies
all buried
in shallow graves?

SONG 3

　　This morning of the small snow
I count the blessings, the leak in the faucet
which makes of the sink time, the drop
of the water on water as sweet
as the Seth Thomas
in the old kitchen
my father stood in his drawers to wind (always
he forgot the 30th day, as I don't want to remember
the rent
　　　　a house these days
so much somebody else's,
especially,
Congoleum's

　　　　Or the plumbing,
that it doesn't work, this I like, have even used paper clips
as well as string to hold the ball up And flush it
with my hand
　　　　But that the car doesn't, that no moving thing moves
without that song I'd void my ear of, the musickracket
of all ownership . . .

                    Holes
in my shoes, that's all right, my fly
gaping, me out
at the elbows, the blessing
                    that difficulties are once more

        "In the midst of plenty, walk
         as close to
         bare
              In the face of sweetness,
         piss
                    In the time of goodness,
         go side, go
         smashing, beat them, go as
         (as near as you can

         tear

         In the land of plenty, have
         nothing to do with it
                         take the way of
         the lowest,
         including
         your legs, go
         contrary, go

         sing

                    SONG 4

I know a house made of mud & wattles,
I know a dress just sewed
                    (saw the wind

blow its cotton
against her body
from the ankle
              so!
it was Nike

And her feet: such bones
I could have had the tears
that lovely pedant had
who couldn't unwrap it himself, had to ask them to,
                                        on the schooner's deck

and he looked,
the first human eyes to look again
at the start of human motion (just last week
300,000,000 years ago

                    She
was going fast
across the square, the water
this time of year, that
scarce

And the fish

SONG 5

I have seen faces of want,
and have not wanted the FAO: Appleseed
's gone back to
what any of us
New England

SONG 6

you sing, you

who also

wants

LOUIS ZUKOVSKY

"It's Hard to See But Think of a Sea"

It's hard to see but think of a sea
Condensed into a speck.
And there are waves—
Frequencies of light,
Others that may be heard.
The one is one sea, the other a second.
There are electric stresses across condensers
That wear them down till they can stand no strain,
Are of no force and as unreclaimed as the bottom of the sea
Unless the space the stresses cross be air, that can be patched.
Large and small condensers,
Passing in the one instance frequencies that can be turned to
        sound,
In the other, alternations that escape,
So many waves of a speck of sea or what,
Or a graph the curve of a wave beyond all sound,
An open circuit where no action—
Like that of the retina made human by light—
Is recorded otherwise
Than having taken a desired path a little way
And tho infinitely a mote to be uncontained for ever.
This science is then like gathering flowers of the weed
One who works with me calls birdseed
That are tiny and many on one stem
They shed to the touch tho on a par with the large flower
That picked will find a vase.
I see many things at one time the harder the concepts get,
Or nothing
Which is a forever become me over forty years.
I am like another, and another, who has finished learning

And has just begun to learn.
If I turn pages back
A child may as well be staring with me
Wondering at the meaning
I turn to last
Perhaps.

"To My Wash-Stand"

To my wash-stand
in which I wash
    my left hand
and my right hand

To my wash-stand
whose base is Greek
    whose shaft
is marble and is fluted

To my wash-stand
whose wash-bowl
    is an oval
in a square

To my wash-stand
whose square is marble
    and inscribes two
smaller ovals to left and right for soap

Comes a song of
water from the right faucet and the left
    my left and my
right hand mixing hot and cold

Comes a flow which
if I have called a song
    is a song
entirely in my head

a song out of imagining
modillions descried above
my head   a frieze
of stone completing what no longer

is my wash-stand
since its marble has completed
my getting up each morning
my washing before going to bed

my look into a mirror
to glimpse half an oval
as if its half
were half-oval in my head   and the

climates of many
inscriptions human heads shapes'
horses' elephants' (tusks) others'
scratched in marble tile

so my wash-stand
in one particular breaking of the
tile at which I have
looked and looked

has opposed to my head
the inscription of a head
whose coinage is the
coinage of the poor

observant in waiting
in their getting up mornings
and in their waiting
going to bed

carefully attentive
to what they have
and to what they do not
have

when a flow of water
     doubled in narrow folds
occasions invertible counterpoints
    over a head   and

an age in a wash-stand
and in their own heads

❧❀❧

GEORGE OPPEN

The Occurrences

The simplest
Words say the grass blade
Hides the blaze
Of a sun
To throw a shadow
In which the bugs crawl
At the roots of the grass;

Father, father
Of fatherhood
Who haunts me, shivering
Man most naked
Of us all, O father

      watch
At the roots
Of the grass the creating
Now   that tremendous
plunge

Resort

There's a volcano snow-capped in the air some twenty miles
    from here
In clear lit air,
There is a tree in leaf here—

In dream an old man walking,
An old man's rounded head
Abruptly mine

Self-involved, strange, alien,
The familiar flesh
Walking. I saw his neck, his cheek

And called, called:
Called several times.

Birthplace: New Rochelle

Returning to that house
And the rounded rocks of childhood—They have lasted well.

A world of things.

An aging man,
The knuckles of my hand
So jointed! I am this?

                                        The house
My father's once, and the ground. There is a color of his
    times
In the sun's light.

A generation's mark.
It intervenes. My child,

Not now a child, our child
Not altogether lone in a lone universe that suffers time
Like stones in sun. For we do not.

Ballad

Astrolabes and lexicons
Once in the great houses—

A poor lobsterman

Met by chance
On Swan's Island

Where he was born
We saw the old farmhouse

Propped and leaning on its hilltop
On that island
Where the ferry runs

A poor lobsterman

His teeth were bad

He drove us over that island
In an old car

A well-spoken man

Hardly real
As he knew in those rough fields

Lobster pots and their gear
Smelling of salt

The rocks outlived the classicists,
The rocks and the lobstermen's huts

And the sights of the island
The ledges in the rough sea seen from the road

And the harbor
And the post office

Difficult to know what one means
—to be serious and to know what one means—

An island
Has a public quality

His wife in the front seat

In a soft dress
Such as poor women wear

She took it that we came—
I don't know how to say, she said—

Not for anything we did, she said,
Mildly, 'from God'. She said

What I like more than anything
Is to visit other islands . . .

~~~~~~

ROBERT CREELEY

~~~~~~~~~~~~~~~~~~~~~~~~~~

The Hill

It is sometime since I have been
to what it was had once turned me backwards,
and made my head into
a cruel instrument.

It is simple
to confess. Then done,
to walk away, walk away,
to come again.

But that form, I must answer,
is dead in me, completely,
and I will not allow it
to reappear—

Saith perversity, the willful,
the magnanimous cruelty,
which is in me
like a hill.

Kore

As I was walking
I came upon
chance walking
the same road upon.

As I sat down
    by chance to move
later
    if and as I might,

light the wood was,
    light and green,
and what I saw
    before I had not seen.

It was a lady
    accompanied
by goat men
    leading her.

Her hair held earth.
    Her eyes were dark.
A double flute
    made her move.

"O love,
    where are you
leading
    me now?"

A Wicker Basket

Comes the time when it's later
and onto your table the headwaiter
puts the bill, and very soon after
rings out the sound of lively laughter—

Picking up change, hands like a walrus,
and a face like a barndoor's,
and a head without an apparent size,
nothing but two eyes—

So that's you, man,
or me. I make it as I can,
I pick up, I go
faster than they know—

Out the door, the street like a night,
any night, and no one in sight,
but then, well, there she is,
old friend Liz—

And she opens the door of her cadillac,
I step in back,
and we're gone.
She turns me on—

There are very huge stars, man, in the sky,
and from somewhere very far off someone hands me a slice of
      apple pie,
with a gob of white, white ice cream on top of it,
and I eat it—

Slowly. And while certainly
they are laughing at me, and all around me is racket
of these cats not making it, I make it

in my wicker basket.

The Joke

There was a joke
went on a walk like
over the hill, and there before them
these weary travellers
saw valleys and farms
of muscles, tits raised high
in the sky of their vision which bewildered
them. They were

no ordinary men but those who come
innocent, late and alone
to women and a home, and keep on talking
and keep on walking.

Dancing

To be a dancer
of my own dismay,
to let my legs and arms
move in their own feeling,

I make a form of assumptions
as real as clothes on a line,
a car moving
that sees another coming,

dancing as all would
were it not for what it thought
it was always doing,
or could leave

itself to itself
whatever it is, dancing,
or better, a jerking leap
toward impulse.

The Birds

for Jane and Stan Brakhage

I'll miss the small birds that come
for the sugar you put out
and the bread crumbs. They've

made the edge of the sea domestic
and, as I am, I welcome that.
Nights my head seemed twisted

with dreams and the sea wash,
I let it all come quiet, waking,
counting familiar thoughts and objects.

Here to rest, like they say, I best
liked walking along the beach
past the town till one reached

the other one, around the corner
of rock and small trees.   It was
clear, and often empty, and

peaceful.   Those lovely ungainly
pelicans fished there, dropping
like rocks, with grace, from the air,

headfirst, then sat on the water,
letting the pouch of their beaks
grow thin again, then swallowing

whatever they'd caught.   The birds,
no matter they're not of our kind,
seem most like us here.   I want

to go where they go, in a way, if
a small and common one.   I want
to ride that air which makes the sea

seem down there, not the element
in which one thrashes to come up.
I love water, I *love* water—

but I also love air, and fire.

Two

Holding
for one
instant this
moment—

*

In mind, in
other places.

LARRY EIGNER

"How Many Times, Death"

How many times,   death
has cried
wolf   the

cloud
   larger than the bay

the ceiling disappears

"Stand on One Foot"

stand on one foot

like a tree

the law
is

    gulls change
    the angle

     air
pressing through leaf
you cannot mount
the green
  sound of

"Lights"

Lights
which go away
  and their reflections
    wet from the street

    cars
  suns given them
pressed bodies streamers goals
      a fume of ships

  the sun a few hours off   right now
necessity coming on sleep   there is this slice of the hill
   between rows like
  a country road
     half minute dark surface this
   day the sun
     stemmed on vacationers
      still arranging night
         the year for
     making it out

"I Have Felt It as They've Said"

I have felt it as they've said
there is nothing to say

there is everything to speak of
   but the words are words

When you speak that is a sound
what have you done, when you have spoken

of nothing
   or something I will remember

   After trying my animal noise
I break out with a man's cry

ROBERT DUNCAN

Sonnet 1

Now there is a Love of which Dante does not speak unkindly,
Tho it grieves his heart to think upon men
   who lust after men and run
      —his beloved Master, Brunetto Latini, among them—
Where the roaring waters of hell's rivers
Come, heard as if muted in the distance,
   like the hum of bees in the hot sun.

Scorcht in whose rays and peeld, these would-be lovers
Turn their faces, peering in the fire-fall,
   to look to one another

As men searching for an other
    in the light of a new moon look.

Sharpening their vision, Dante says, like a man
    seeking to thread a needle,
They try the eyes of other men
Towards that eye of the needle
    Love has appointed there
For a joining that is not easy.

Sonnet 2

    For it is as if the thread of my life
    had been wedded to the eye of its needle.

    In the sunlight his head
    bends over his sewing,

    intent upon joining color to color,
    working the bedclothes of many cloths.

    This patch of Dante's vision in like art
    he keeps in Love's name and unites

    to the treasured remnant of some velvet shirt.
    The flames of the river coupled with the velvet

    illustrate the household scene.
    He makes it up as he goes along.

    It is as if our lives in one thread
    had entered the eye of a lasting need

    to begin this work, for this Love
    of whom I speak

    is not the angel Amor of Dante's song,
    tho in him we remember Amor,

but a worker among men
who has taken our lives as one thread

to join as if again
what we see in what we have never seen.

❦

DENISE LEVERTOV

Our Bodies

Our bodies, still young under
the engraved anxiety of our
faces, and innocently

more expressive than faces:
nipples, navel, and pubic hair
make anyway a

sort of face: or taking
the rounded shadows at
breast, buttock, balls,

the plump of my belly, the
hollow of your
groin, as a constellation,

how it leans from earth to
dawn in a gesture of
play and

wise compassion—
nothing like this
comes to pass

in eyes or wistful
mouths.
                    I have

a line or groove I love
runs down
my body from breastbone
to waist. It speaks of
eagerness, of
distance.

            Your long back,
the sand color and
how the bones show, say

what sky after sunset
almost white
over a deep woods to which

rooks are homing, says.

ROBERT KELLY

Poem for Easter

All women are beautiful as they rise
exultant from the ruins they make of us

& this woman
who lies back informing the sheets

has slain me with all day love & now
keeps vigil at the tomb of my desire

from which also she will make me rise
& come before her into galilee

Rising I fall
& what does her beauty matter

except it is a darkness sabbath
where the church—our bodies

everywhere come together—
kindles one small light

from the unyielding the flint
then resurrection

The radio Messiah
I know

that my redeemer liveth
& he shall stand in the last days

up from this earth
beyond blasphemy

beyond misunderstanding
O love this hour will not let me name

they will say I make
a sexual mystery of your passion

whereas we know
flesh rises

to apprehend one other mystery
as the lover's

astonished eyes come open in his coming
to find that he is not alone

❧

~~~~~~~~~~~~~~~~~~~~~~~~~~~~~~

GARY SNYDER

~~~~~~~~~~~~~~~~~~~~

For a Stone Girl at Sanchi

half asleep on the cold grass
    night rain flicking the maples
under a black bowl upside-down
on a flat land
      on a wobbling speck
smaller than stars,
    space,
  the size of a seed,
    hollow as bird skulls,
light flies across it
    —never is seen.

a big rock weathered funny,
 old tree trunks turnd stone,
    split rocks and find clams.
     all that time
loving:
  two flesh persons changing,
    clung to, doorframes
    notions, spear-hafts
in a rubble of years.
     touching.
this dream pops. it was real:
    and it lasted forever.

Nansen

I found you on a rainy morning
After a typhoon
In a bamboo grove at Daitoku-ji.
Tiny wet rag with a
Huge voice, you crawled under the fence
To my hand. Left to die.
I carried you home in my raincoat.
"Nansen, cheese!" you'd shout an answer
And come running.
But you never got big.
Bandy-legged bright little dwarf—
Sometimes not eating, often coughing
Mewing bitterly at inner twinge.

Now, thin and older, you won't eat
But milk and cheese. Sitting on a pole
In the sun. Hardy with resigned
Discontent.
You just weren't made right. I saved you.
And your three-year life has been full
Of mild, steady pain.

Thief

About when the stars of the Skeleton
        were paling in the dawn:
Striding the crackly glitter
        —frozen mud—
The thief who had just stolen a celadon vase
        from the front of a store
Suddenly stopped those long black legs
Covered his ears with his hands
And listened to the humming of his mind.

KENNETH REXROTH

The Mirror in the Woods

A mirror hung on the broken
Walls of an old summer house
Deep in the dark woods. Nothing
Ever moved in it but the
Undersea shadows of ferns,
Rhododendrons and redwoods.
Moss covered the frame. One day
The gold and glue gave way and
The mirror slipped to the floor.
For many more years it stood
On the shattered boards. Once in
A long time a wood rat would
Pass it by without ever
Looking in. At last we came,
Breaking the sagging door and
Letting in a narrow wedge
Of sunlight. We took the mirror
Away and hung it in my
Daughter's room with a barre before
It. Now it reflects ronds, escartes,
Relevés and arabesques.
In the old house the shadows,
The wood rats and moss work unseen.

KENNETH PATCHEN

The Origin of Baseball

Someone had been walking in and out
Of the world without coming
To much decision about anything.
The sun seemed too hot most of the time.
There weren't enough birds around
And the hills had a silly look
When he got on top of one.
The girls in heaven, however, thought
Nothing of asking to see his watch
Like you would want someone to tell
A joke—"Time," they'd say, "what's
That mean—time?", laughing with the edges
Of their white mouths, like a flutter of paper
In a madhouse. And he'd stumble over
General Sherman or Elizabeth B.
Browning, muttering, "Can't you keep
Your big wings out of the aisle?" But down
Again, there'd be millions of people without
Enough to eat and men with guns just
Standing there shooting each other.

So he wanted to throw something
And he picked up a baseball.

KENNETH FEARING

Art Review

Recently displayed at the Times Square Station, a new Van
    dyke on the face-cream girl.
(Artist unknown. Has promise, but lacks the brilliance show
    by the great masters of the Elevated age)
The latest wood carving in a Whelan telephone booth, title
    "O Mortal Fools WA 9-5090," shows two winged hear
    above an ace of spades.
(His meaning is not entirely clear, but this man will go far)
A charcoal nude in the rear of Flatbush Ahearn's Bar & Gril
    "Forward to the Brotherhood of Man," has been bold
    conceived in the great tradition.
(We need more, much more of this)
Then there is the chalk portrait, on the walls of a waterfront
    warehouse, of a gentleman wearing a derby hat: "Bleec
    er Street Mike is a doublecrossing rat."
(Morbid, but powerful. Don't miss)

Know then by these presents, know all men by these signs an
    omens, by these simple thumbprints on the throat of tim
Know that Pete, the people's artist, is ever watchful,
That Tuxedo Jim has passed among us, and was much di
    pleased, as always,
That George the Ghost (no man has ever seen him) an
    Billy the Bicep boy will neither bend nor break,
That Mr. Harkness of Sunnyside still hopes for the best, an
    has not lost his human touch,
That Phantom Phil, the master of them all, has come an
    gone, but will return, and all is well.

How Do I Feel?

Get this straight, Joe, and don't get me wrong.
Sure, Steve, O.K., all I got to say is, when do I get the dough?

Will you listen for a minute? And just shut up? Let a guy explain?
Go ahead, Steve, I won't say a word.

Will you just shut up?
O.K., I tell you, whatever you say, it's O.K. with me.

What's O.K. about it, if that's the way you feel?
What do you mean, how I feel? What do you know, how I feel?

Listen, Joe, a child could understand, if you'll listen for a minute without butting in, and don't get so sore.
Sure, I know, you got to collect it first before you lay it out, I know that; you can't be left on a limb yourself.

Me? On a limb? For a lousy fifty bucks?
Take it easy, Steve, I'm just saying—

I'm just telling you—
Wait, listen—

Now listen, wait, will you listen for a minute? That's all I ask. Yes or no?
O.K., I only—

Yes or no?
O.K., O.K.

O.K., then, and you won't get sore? If I tell it to you straight?
Sure, Steve, O.K., all I got to say is, when do I get the dough?

Jack Knuckles Falters

*(But Reads Own Statement at His Execution
While Wardens Watch)*

HAS LITTLE TO SAY
Gentlemen, I
Feel there is little I
Care to say at this moment, but the reporters have urged that
Express a few appropriate remarks.

THANKS WARDEN FOR KINDNESS
I am grateful to Warden E. J. Springer for the many kind
    nesses he has shown me in the last six months,
And I also wish to thank my friends who stuck by me to th
    last.
As one who entered his nation's defense

STAGGERS WHEN HE SEES ELECTRIC CHAIR
Five days after war was declared, I was hoping for a pardo
    from the governor,
But evidently the government has forgotten its veterans i
    their moment of need.
What brought me to the chair

WILL RUMANIAN PRINCE WED AGAIN?
Was keeping bad companions against the advice of my moth
    and companions.
How I

WISHES HE COULD HAVE ANOTHER CHANCE
Wish I could live my life over again. If I
Could only be given another chance I would show the worl
    how to be a man, but I

"I AM AN INNOCENT MAN," DECLARES KNUCKLE
Declare before God gentlemen that I am an innocent man,
As innocent as any of you now standing before me, and th
    final sworn word I

POSITIVE IDENTIFICATION CLINCHED KNUCKLES
    VERDICT
Publish to the world is that I was framed. I
Never saw the dead man in all my life, did not know about the
    killing until

BODY PLUNGES AS CURRENT KILLS
My arrest, and I
Swear to you with my last breath that I
Was not on the corner of Lexington and Fifty-ninth streets
    at eight o'clock.
SEE U.S. INVOLVED IN FISHERY DISPUTE
EARTHQUAKE REPORTED IN PERU

CHARLES BUKOWSKI

The Tragedy of the Leaves

I awakened to dryness and the ferns were dead
the potted plants yellow as corn;
my woman was gone
and the empty bottles like bled corpses
surrounded me with their uselessness;
the sun was still good, though,
and my landlady's note cracked in fine and
undemanding yellowness; what was needed now
was a good comedian, ancient style, a jester
with jokes upon absurd pain; pain is absurd
because it exists, nothing more;
I shaved carefully with an old razor
the man who had once been young and
said to have genius; but
that's the tragedy of the leaves,

the dead ferns, the dead plants;
and I walked into the dark hall
where the landlady stood
execrating and final,
sending me to hell,
waving her fat sweaty arms
and screaming
screaming for rent
because the world had failed us
both.

Riot

the reason for the riot was we kept getting beans
and a guard grabbed a colored boy who threw his
on the floor
and somebody touched a button
and everybody was grabbing everybody;
I clubbed my best friend behind the ear,
somebody threw coffee in my face
(what the hell, you couldn't drink it)
and I got out to the yard
and I heard the guns going
and it seemed like every con had a knife but me,
and all I could do was pray and run
and I didn't have a god and was fat from playing
poker for pennies with my cellmate,
and the warden's voice started coming over the cans,
and I heard later, in the confusion,
the cook raped a sailor,
and I lost my shaving cream, a pack of smokes
and a copy of the *New Yorker;*
also 3 men were shot,
a half-dozen knifed,
55 put in the hole,
all yard privileges suspended,
the screws as jittery as L. A. bookies,
the prison radio off,

real quiet,
visitors sent home,
but the next morning
we did get our mail—
a letter from St. Louis:
Dear Charles, I am sorry you are in prison,
but you cannot break the law,
and there was a pressed carnation,
perfume, the looming of panties,
laughter and beer,
and that night for dinner
they marched us all back down
to the beans.

CHRISTOPHER LOGUE

"Where Have You Been?"

Where have you been?
I've been to the dance.

Where did you stay?
I stayed with a man.

You'll have to get married.
He's married already.

Your daughter is right.
The sergeant is married.

She's got to be punished.

She's washing her hair.

Your mother and I
have decided to drive
you and your dog to the desert.
When we find the right place
you'll shoot your dog.
Now go to bed.

I've set the clock.
We must teach her a lesson.

"He Lived Near Here"

He lived near here.
Before the war most people couldn't read.

My father came in with the paper
and this is what he said
Fetch Mary.

She came in her blue.

There were four strange men in the room.
They looked in the tea my mother had made.
Read it, he said.

She was nine. We had the same stars.

And the article said
how a man had committed the act with his eldest
and when it was due he took her by tube
and the hospital was the one facing Parliament
and on his first visit he grabbed up the child
and ran past the nurses
and out of the place
and down to the river
and threw it right in.

My father gave Mary a penny for reading.
He smoked forty a day and got killed in the war.

You remember that man they hanged for the drowning?
my mother asked fifteen years later.

Mary had moved. I still have her card.

We knew him.
His wife died of something. His eldest kept house.
She came here the evening they took him away.

If ever I go to a dance with Yvonne
—the loose one who bit herself off when the Yankees went
        home—
when I get back he is waiting.
He strips me and has me downstairs.
When he's finished he says
What you give to them you'll give me too.

Except for this he's kind.
He calls me our mother
and gives me his wages unopened.

The funny thing is
no one had it save him.
Well, maybe a feel, but no more.

"O Come All Ye Faithful"

O come all ye faithful
here is our cause,
all dreams are one dream,
all wars civil wars.

Lovers have never found
agony strange,

we who hate change survive
only through change.

Those who are sure of love
do not complain,
for sure of love is sure
love comes again.

ANSELM HOLLO

Minotaur Poem

½ human, ½ bull

To say good morning blues how do you do
something is sneaking around the corner
not about the weather
myself I'm feeling pretty bad
not about the climate
you are adorable
but of certain limitations
myself I'll go to spain one of these days
but of no importance
all of you are wonderful people
and to say it is a great pleasure indeed
with a lilt

GEORGE MacBETH

A Riddle

for Ponge

I

It is always handled
with a certain

caution. After all,
it is present

on so many private
occasions. It goes

into all our darkest
corners. It accepts

a continual
diminution of itself

in the act
of moving, receiving

only a touch
in return. If a girl

lays it along
her cheek, it eases

the conscience. It salves
the raw wound,

nipping it clean. To be
so mobile

and miss nothing
it has to be

soft. It is.

II

Consider
the pornography

of its
nightly progress. It moves

between our legs
like a ghost

lover, melting
into essence before

those
elaborate organs. As

underwater
flowers, they close

against it. So
many

resistances, such
rich

anticipations!

III

It is like
ourselves, malleable,

strange-smelling,
subject to the hands

of women in
so many postures. We

take it to our skin
in thin

layers of itself,
our image. It

loves water
as we do. In that

the bean-stalk
riots

as lovingly
as a dolphin. In

that
it lives, easing

its whole
body, unto

death, slowly.

[G.M.] The answer is: a piece of soap.

❧ⴺ⌘⌘ⴻ☙

EDWARD FIELD

Sweet Gwendolyn and the Countess

The Countess rode out on her black horse in spring
wearing her black leather riding costume.
She was scouting for disciples in the countryside
and flicked with her whip the rosebuds as she passed.

Sweet Gwendolyn in her white dress
was out gathering May flowers.
Under sunshade hat, her pale face
blushed to the singing bees,
and her golden curls lay passive on bent shoulders
as she stooped to pluck a white lily.

The Countess passing by took one look,
galloped up, and reined her stallion sharply in,
high over the modest figure
of Sweet Gwendolyn with the downcast eyes.
She leaped down from her horse and knelt,
laying the whip in tribute before the golden girl.

That foolish one swooned forward to the ground
in a great white puff of dress fabric
and a scattering of flowers. At that,
the Countess rose in all her black pride
and put her dirty leather boot hard on Gwendolyn's bent neck,
pushing down the golden head to the grass,
and gave her a smart lash across her innocently upturned
    behind.

Gwendolyn looked up with begging eyes
and a small whimper of submission,

as the Countess pushed her over and threw the skirt up,
exposing legs and bottom bare,
and shoved the leather whip handle between squeezed thighs
    of virtue
forcing them apart to reveal the pink pulsing maidenhood.

Poor Gwendolyn moaned with shame and pain
as she lay back crushing her Mayflowers, exposed and un-
    resisting—
until the Countess, in full charge, pulled her to her feet,
tied the whip end around her neck,
remounted the big black horse
and slowly trotted off,
leading the sobbing girl a captive behind her
off to her dark castle.

GREGORY CORSO

The Mad Yak

I am watching them churn the last milk
    they'll ever get from me.
They are waiting for me to die;
They want to make buttons out of my bones.
Where are my sisters and brothers?
That tall monk there, loading my uncle,
    he has a new cap.
And that idiot student of his—
    I never saw that muffler before.
Poor uncle, he lets them load him.
How sad he is, how tired!

I wonder what they'll do with his bones?
And that beautiful tail!
How many shoelaces will they make of that!

Seed Journey

There they go
and where they stop
trees will grow

The nuts of amnesiac squirrels
more nuts will be
Bur takes freight on animal fur
And pollen the wind does carry

For some seeds
meal is the end of the journey

A Dreamed Realization

The carrion-eater's nobility calls back from God;
Never was a carrion-eater *first* a carrion-eater—
Back there in God creatures sat like stone
—no light in their various eyes.

Life. It was Life jabbed a spoon in their mouths.
Crow jackal hyena vulture worm woke to necessity
—dipping into Death like a soup.

ALLEN GINSBERG

Describe: The Rain on Dasaswamedh

Kali Ma tottering up steps to shelter tin roof, feeling her way
        to curb, around bicycle & leper seated on her way—to
        piss on a broom
left by the Stone Cutters who last night were shaking the
        street with Boom! of Stone blocks unloaded from truck
Forcing the blindman in his grey rags to retreat from his spot
        in the middle of the road where he sleeps & shakes under
        his blanket
Jai Ram all night telling his beads or sex on a burlap carpet
Past which cows donkeys dogs camels elephants marriage
        processions drummers tourists lepers and bathing devotees
step to the whine of serpent-pipes & roar of car motors around
        his black ears—
Today on a balcony in shorts leaning on iron rail I watched
        the leper who sat hidden behind a bicycle
emerge dragging his buttocks on the grey rainy ground by the
        glove-bandaged stumps of hands,
one foot chopped off below knee, round stump-knob wrapped
        with black rubber
pushing a tin can shiny size of his head with left hand (from
        which only a thumb emerged from leprous swathings)
beside him, lifting it with both ragbound palms down the curb
        into the puddled road,
balancing his body down next to the can & crawling forward
        on his behind
trailing a heavy rag for seat, and leaving a path thru the street
        wavering
like the Snail's slime track—imprint of his crawl on the muddy
        asphalt market entrance—stopping

to drag his can along stubbornly konking on the paved surfa
    near the water pump—

Where a turban'd workman stared at him moving along—h
    back humped with rags—

and inquired why didn't he put his can to wash in the pun
    altarplace—and why go that way when free rice

Came from the alley back there by the river—As the lep
    looked up & rested, conversing curiously, can by his si
    approaching a puddle.

Kali had pissed standing up & then felt her way back to tl
    Shop Steps on thin brown legs

her hands in the air—feeling with feet for her rag pile on tl
    stone steps' wetness—

as a cow busied its mouth chewing her rags left wet on tl
    ground for five minutes digesting

Till the comb-&-hair-oil-booth keeper woke & chased her awa
    with a stick

Because a dog barked at a madman with dirty wild black ha
    who rag round his midriff & water pot in hand

Stopped in midstreet turned round & gazed up at the balconie
    windows, shops and city stagery filled with glum activi

Shrugged & said *Jai Shankar!* to the imaginary audience
    Me's.

While a white robed Baul Singer carrying his one stringe
    dried pumpkin Guitar

Sat down near the cigarette stand and surveyed his new scen
    just arrived in the Holy City of Benares.

PHILIP LAMANTIA

Hypodermic Light

It's absurd I can't bring my soul to the eye of odoriferous fire

my soul whose teeth never leave their cadavers
my soul twisted on rocks of mental freeways
my soul that hates music
I would rather not see the Rose in my thoughts take on
    illusionary prerogatives
it is enough to have eaten bourgeois testicles
it is enough that the masses are all sodomites
Good Morning
the ships are in I've brought the gold to burn Moctezuma
I'm in a tipi joking with seers I'm smoking yahnah
I'm in a joint smoking marijuana with a cat who looks like
    Jesus Christ
heroin is a door always opened by white women
my first act of treason was to be born!
I'm at war with the Zodiac
my suffering comes on as a fire going out O beautiful world
    contemplation!

It's a fact my soul is smoking!

◻

That the total hatred wants to annihilate me!
it's the sickness of american pus against which I'm hallucinated
I'm sick of language
I want this wall I see under my eyes break up and shatter you
I'm talking all the poems after God
I want the table of visions to send me oriole opium

A state of siege
It's possible to live directly from elementals! hell stamps ou
    vegetable spirits, zombies attack heaven! the marvelou
    put down by martial law, America fucked by a stick o
    marijuana
paper money larded for frying corpses!

HERE comes the Gorgon! THERE'S the outhouse!

      Come up from dead things, anus of the sun!

□

old after midnight spasm
juke box waits for junk
round about midnight music
combing bop hair
getting ready to cook
Jupiter wails!
heroins of visionary wakeup in light of Bird and The Going
    Forth By Day
the pipe's spiritual brain winters off the Nile old hypodermic
    needle under foot of Anubis
                Mother Death
I'm at the boat of Ra Set
I'm Osiris hunting stars his black tail of the sun!
It's the end of melancholy   sad   bop   midnights

□

They shot me full of holes at Kohlema's hut!
It's you who'll be butchered in my precise imagination
It'll be hard to withstand the reasoning of peyotl Rack

    many times my song went downstairs, people of entire
    hate
and I burned you in basements without tearing my face up
O people I hate the most! glass automobiles snake by to decay
    decay is living anthill
where yr automobiles lift their skirts and stiff

pricks of dead indians going in reverse
automobile graveyards where I eat fenders, bodies I crunch
mustards of engines I devour whole gallons of molding
chrome I whip cheese from cannibal hoods

O beautiful people of hate! your money fenders how creamy!
your electric eyes stinking! your geometric reconstructions
against my destructions!

❦

LEROI JONES

A Poem Some People
Will Have to Understand

Dull unwashed windows of eyes
and buildings of industry. What
industry do I practice? A slick
colored boy, 12 miles from his
home. I practice no industry.
I am no longer a credit
to my race. I read a little,
scratch against silence slow spring
afternoons.

    I had thought, before, some years ago
that I'd come to the end of my life.

    Water color ego. Without the preciseness
a violent man could propose.

    But the wheel, and the wheels,
won't let us alone. All the fantasy
and justice, and dry charcoal winters

All the pitifully intelligent citizens
        I've forced myself
to love.
    We have awaited the coming of a natural
    phenomenon. Mystics and romantics, knowledgeable
    workers
    of the land.

    But none has come.
    (REPEAT)
        but none has come.
Will the machinegunners please step forward?

JACK KEROUAC

120th Chorus

    Junkies that get too high
    Shoot up their old stock of stuff
    And sit stupidly on edge
    Of bed nodding over
    The single sentence in the paper
        They been staring at all night—
        Six, seven hours they'll do this,
        Or get hungup on paragraphs:

    "You go on the nod,
        Then you come up,
            Then you start readin
            it again
        Then you go on the nod again
        and everytime you read it
            it gets better"

You dont remember the next
          rebirth
      but you remember
        the experience

"Took me all evening to read
3 or 4 pages, ossified,
on the nod"

201st Chorus

When the girls start puttin
          Nirvana-No on their lips
Nobody'll see them.
          Poor girls, did they always
Want attention? Did they
          always disturb
The sitting saint in the woods
          and make him feel
Cheap by sayin: "Those
          guys think they
can sit down & be God."
—"They think they dont
     have to work
     because they are God
     and they sit down
     and think they are God"
     —Those Guys . . .
Over their heads is the unbelievable
                    unending
                    emptiness
                    the enormous
                    nothingness
                    of the skies
     And they claim

MICHAEL McCLURE

THE STARS ARE A SHIELD OF NOTHING
CREATED OF NOTHING
AND I CALL ON THEE TO SWING,
ashahh harr marrr gahrooo yahr aye-howw tanthor rahrr
ooohmah thownie toww smeels tor sheen
thah gahreems wooven mah laughter eehn nroh
beyond the final first devi now shemetter
poor ahn gras nowerhoww hayrayoar
bleth tomakayne grahhr shageer
raise up thy heeze ahn streee entoh eeze.
LOOK UP!
See our calm, titanic, minuscule gestures.
YAHRR NOH. HRAHHHRR-NOHH!

EUGEN GOMRINGER

words are shadows
shadows become words

words are games
games become words

are shadows words
do words become games

are games words
do words become shadows

are words shadows
do games become words

are words games
do shadows become words

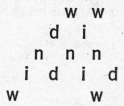

silence silence silence
silence silence silence
silence   silence
silence silence silence
silence silence silence

schif schif schif schif schif schif
fihcs fihcs fihcs fihcs fihcs fihcs
hcsif hcsif hcsif hcsif hcsif hcsif
fisch fisch fisch fisch fisch fisch

fisch fisch fisch fisch fisch fisch
hcsif hcsif hcsif hcsif hcsif hcsif
fisch fisch fisch fisch fisch fisch
schif schif schif schif schif schif
fihcs fihcs fihcs fihcs fihcs fihcs

fisch = fish
schif(f) = boat

SEIICHI NIIKUNI

川 = river
州 = sandbank

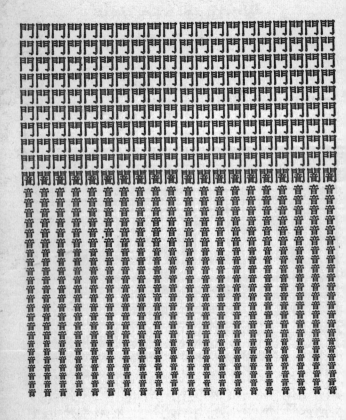

門 = door
闇 = obscurity
音 = sound

DÉCIO PIGNATARI

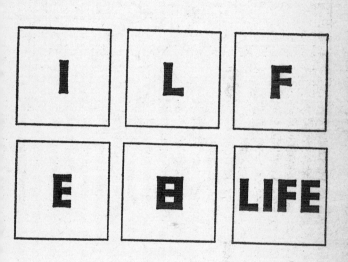

~~~~~~~~~~~~~~~~~~~~~~~~~~~~~~~~~~~~~~

PEDRO XISTO

~~~~~~~~~~~~~~~~~~~~~~~~~~~~~~~~~~~~~~

Epithalamium II

he = ele   S = serpens
& = e   h = homo
she = ela   e = eva

LADISLAV NOVAK

O

GL RIA

REINHARD DÖHL

Wurm in Apfel

ApfelApfelApfelApfel
ApfelApfelApfelApfelApfelA
ApfelApfelApfelApfelApfe
ApfelApfelApfelApfelApfelApf
ApfelApfelApfelApfelApfelApfel
ApfelApfelApfelApfelApfelApfe
ApfelApfelApfelApfelApfelApfelA
ApfelApfelApfelApfelApfelApfe
ApfelApfelApfelApfelApfelApfel
ApfelApfelApfelApfelApfelApf
ApfelApfelApfelWurmApf
ApfelApfelApfelApfel
ApfelApfelApfelA
ApfelApfelA
ApfelApfel

IAN HAMILTON FINLAY

"A little burn (stream) flows with a sound which suggests tunes on a mouth-organ. Its path is denoted by the x's and m's, the m's being the sound and the x's a windmill, as well as the conventional sign for kisses—of light on water, perhaps—and signs of happiness. Different sizes and kinds of type suggest the altering nature of the water." (I.H.F.)

```
                    m
                   Mm
                    x
                    m
                  mMm
                    x
                    m
                   mm
                  m
                   mm
                    x
              MmM
              mm
              m
              m
              mm
             m
              x
            mmm
            m
              m
            mm
              x
              m
               mmMm
               m
                x
               m
               mm
               m
               this
               is
               the
               little
               burn
              that
             plays
             its
             mm
           mMm
           m
          mmouth-
          organ
            by
            the
            m
            mm
             mmm
             mMm
             mill
              x
             mm
            Mmm
```

A

... blue boat
a brown sail

LITTLE

a brown boat
a green sail

TO PUT

a green boat
a black sail

YOUR EYES

a black boat
a blue sail

TO SLEEP

a...

LITTLE...

acrobats

a   a   a   a   a
  c   c   c   c
r   r   r   r   r
  o   o   o   o
b   b   b   b   b
  a   a   a   a
t   t   t   t   t
  s   s   s   s
t   t   t   t   t
  a   a   a   a
b   b   b   b   b
  o   o   o   o
r   r   r   r   r
  c   c   c   c
a   a   a   a   a

redboat

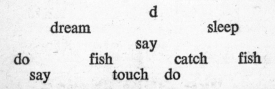

redboatredboatredboatredboatredboatredboat
bedboatbedboatbedboatbedboatbedboatbedboat

<pre>
                         d
        dream   sleep
                        say
      do   fish   catch   fish
        say   touch   do
</pre>

bedboatbedboatbedboatbedboatbedboatbedboat
redboatredboatredboatredboatredboatredboat

EMMETT WILLIAMS

like   attracts   like
like   attracts   like
like   attracts   like
like   attracts   like
like   attracts   like
like   attracts   like
like attracts like
likeattractslike
likeattractlike
likeattractlike
liketraclike
likteralilke
likelikts

~~~~~~~~~~~~~~~~~~~~~~~~~~~~

RONALDO AZEREDO

~~~~~~~~~~~~~~~~~~

```
VVVVVVVVV
VVVVVVVVE
VVVVVVVEL
VVVVVVVELO
VVVVVVELOC
VVVVVELOCI
VVVVELOCID
VVVELOCIDA
VVELOCIDAD
VELOCIDADE
```

RONALD JOHNSON

Maze (with Moon) of Three Minds

~~~~~~~~~~~~~~~~~~~~~~~~~~~~~~

ARAM SAROYAN

~~~~~~~~~~~~~~~~~~~~~~

wwww

wwww

. . . .

waww

wakw

wake

. . . .

walw

walk

MARY ELLEN SOLT

Forsythia

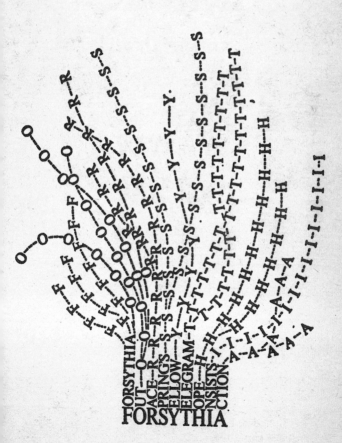

Wild Crab

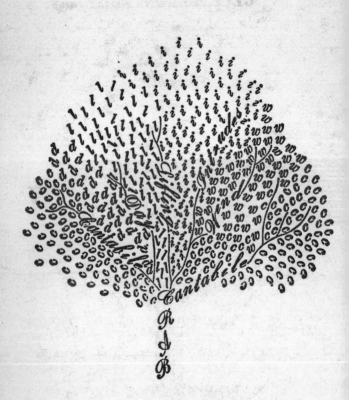

Wind, Intrudes, Lifting Day,
Cantabile, cantabile,

JONATHAN WILLIAMS

Uncle Iv Surveys His Domain
from His Rocker of a Sunday Afternoon
as Aunt Dory Starts to Chop Kindling

Mister Williams
lets youn me move
tother side the house

the woman
choppin woods
mite nigh the awkerdist thing
I seen

From Uncle Jake Carpenter's Anthology
of Death on Three-Mile Creek

Loney Ollis
age 84
dide jun 10 1871

grates dere honter
wreked bee trees for hony
cild ratell snak by 100
cild dere by thousen

i nod him well

Lee Ogle Ties a Broom & Ponders
Cures for Arthuritis

lands them fingers really
dreadfulled me I
couldnt tie
nary broom one

had to soak em in water
hot as birds blood

then I heared this ol man from Kentucky say
take a jug of apple juice just juice not cider
pour the epsum salts to it and
take as much as you kin

bein fleshy I kin take
right smart but
boys you know it moves a mans bowels
somethin terrible

well boys it just
naturally killed that arthuritis
lost me some weight too
and I
still tie thesehere brooms

pretty good

The Custodian of a Field of Whisky Bushes
By the Nolichucky River Speaks:

took me a pecka real ripe tomaters up
into the Grassy Gap
one night

and two quarts of good stockade
and just laid there

sippin and tastin and lookin agin the moon
at them sort of fish eyes in the jar
you get when its right

boys Im talkin bout somethin
good

RUSSELL EDSON

A Stone Is Nobody's

A man ambushed a stone. Caught it. Made it a prisoner. Put it in a dark room and stood guard over it for the rest of his life.

His mother asked why.

He said, because it's held captive, because it is the captured.

Look, the stone is asleep, she said, it does not know whether it's in a garden or not. Eternity and the stone are mother and daughter; it is you who are getting old. The stone is only sleeping.

But I caught it, mother, it is mine by conquest, he said.

A stone is nobody's, not even its own. It is you who are conquered; you are minding the prisoner, which is yourself, because you are afraid to go out, she said.

Yes yes, I am afraid, because you have never loved me, he said.

Which is true, because you have always been to me as the stone is to you, she said.

The Fight

A man is fighting with a cup of coffee. The rules: He must not break the cup nor spill its coffee; nor must the cup break the man's bones or spill his blood.

The man said, oh the hell with it, as he swept the cup to the floor. The cup did not break but its coffee poured out of its open self.

The cup cried, don't hurt me, please don't hurt me; I am without mobility, I have no defense save my utility; use me to hold your coffee.

An Animal, or What Happened
in a Wood

A large animal killed an old man in the wood one day. The animal put on the old man's clothes. The animal did not know how to tie the laces on an old man's shoes. It did not matter. Nothing matters now. The animal put one of the old man's shoes on its head, and his hat on one of its feet. But, that as it walked grew weary of having its foot in the hat, and with rage kicked it away.

The hat landed on a turtle. The turtle found itself isolated and in darkness, surrounded by human odor. At first it felt that the hat must be a human stomach, and that it was swallowed. But seeing that it was not dead nor in pain, and that it could move even with this human burden, it continued. And so a man's hat was seen moving slowly in a wood.

The animal came to a house. An old woman came out and started to beat the animal, screaming, where is your father?

Dead Daughter

Wake up, I heard something die, said a woman to something else.

Something else was her father. Do not call me something else, he said.

Will it be something dead for breakfast? said the woman.

It is always something dead given by your mother to her husband, said her father, like my dead daughter, dead inside herself; there is nothing living there, no heart, no child.

That is not true, said the daughter, I am in here trying to live, but afraid to come out.

If you're in there oh do come out, we're having a special treat, dead daughter for breakfast, dead daughter for lunch, and dead daughter for supper, in fact dead daughter for the rest of our lives.

Waiting for the Signal Man

A woman said to her mother, where is my daughter?

Her mother said, up you and through me and out of grandmother; coming all the way down through all women like a railway train, trailing her brunette hair, which streams back grey into white; waiting for the signal man to raise his light so she can come through.

What she waiting for? said the woman.

For the signal man to raise his light, so she can see to come through.

❧

RICHARD BRAUTIGAN

November 3

I'm sitting in a cafe,
drinking a Coke.

A fly is sleeping
on a paper napkin.

I have to wake him up,
so I can wipe my glasses.

There's a pretty girl
I want to look at.

Mating Saliva

A girl in a green mini-
skirt, not very pretty, walks
  down the street.

A businessman stops, turns
to stare at her ass
that looks like a moldy
  refrigerator.

There are now 200,000,000 people
  in America.

A Mid-February Sky Dance

Dance toward me, please, as
if you were a star
with light-years piled
on top of your hair,
    smiling,

and I will dance toward you
as if I were darkness
with bats piled like a hat
    on top of my head.

Romeo and Juliet

If you will die for me,
I will die for you

and our graves will
be like two lovers washing
their clothes together
in a laundromat.

If you will bring the soap,
I will bring the bleach.

As the Bruises Fade, the Lightning Aches

As the bruises fade, the lightning aches.
Last week, making love, you bit me.
Now the blue and dark have gone
and yellow bruises grow toward pale daffodils,
then paler to become until my body
is all my own and what that ever got me.

To England

There are no postage stamps that send letters
back to England three centuries ago,
no postage stamps that make letters
travel back until the grave hasn't been dug yet,
and John Donne stands looking out the window,
it is just beginning to rain this April morning,
and the birds are falling into the trees
like chess pieces into an unplayed game,
and John Donne sees the postman coming up the street,
the postman walks very carefully because his cane
is made of glass.

BILL KNOTT

Sleep

We brush the other, invisible moon.
Its caves come out and carry us inside.

Prosepoem

Each evening the sea casts starfish up on the beach, scattering,
stranding them. They die at dawn, leaving black hungers in
the sun. We slept there that summer, we fucked in their
radiant evolutions up to our body. Ringed by starfish gasping
for their element, we joined to create ours. All night they

aled the sweat from our thrusting limbs, and lived. Often
cried out: Your hand! —It was a starfish, caressing her
h my low fire.

Hair Poem

Hair is heaven's water flowing eerily over us
Often a woman drifts off down her long hair and is lost

Death

Going to sleep, I cross my hands on my chest.
They will place my hands like this.
It will look as though I am flying into myself.

Poem

for Marion Helz

When our hands are alone,
they open, like faces.
There is no shore
to their opening.

~~~~~~

JAMES TATE

~~~~~~~~~~~~~~~~~~~~~

Rape in the Engineering Building

What I saw on his face scared me—ants
on jelly; two cars ducked as he zigzagged

past the library up to the tracks
where the other students were just falling

from classes. One big man yelled,
stop him stop that man, but I thought

it was personal and got out of their
way. Finally the aproned man told us

in a high stuck voice it was rape
in the engineering building, and

the rapist was chugging farther up
the inclined edge of town into

the shadowy upright garden.
Full of thanks, we took after him.

Leaving Mother Waiting for Father

The evening went on;
I got very old.
She kept telling me it didn't matter.
The real man would come back
soon. We waited. We had alarms

fixed, vases of white and purple
flowers ready to thrust
on him should he.

We had to sell the place
in a hurry; walked downtown
holding hands.
She had a yard of blue material in her pocket:
I remember that so well!
She fell asleep and a smile
began to blister her old mouth.
I propped her against a hotel
and left without any noise.

Dark Street

So this is the dark street
where only an angel lives:
I never saw anything like it.
For the first time in a lifetime
I feel the burgeoning of wings
somewhere behind my frontal lobes.
So this is the dark street.
Did his lights come on,
or do I dream?
I never saw anything like it.

Even the trees' languorous leaves
look easy to touch.
So this is the dark street.
Here he comes now:
good afternoon, Father—
your handshake is so pleasing.
Brush the shards from my shoulders,
what lives we have ahead of us!
So this is the dark street.
I never saw anything like it.

〜〜〜〜〜〜〜〜〜〜〜〜〜〜〜〜〜〜〜〜〜〜

MARK STRAND

〜〜〜〜〜〜〜〜〜〜〜〜〜

The Marriage

The wind comes from opposite poles,
traveling slowly.

She turns in the deep air.
He walks in the clouds.

She readies herself,
shakes out her hair,

makes up her eyes,
smiles.

The sun warms her teeth,
the tip of her tongue moistens them.

He brushes the dust from his suit
and straightens his tie.

He smokes.
Soon they will meet.

The wind carries them closer.
They wave.

Closer, closer.
They embrace.

She is making a bed.
He is pulling off his pants.

They marry
and have a child.

The wind carries them off
in different directions.

The wind is strong, he thinks
as he straightens his tie.

I like this wind, she says
as she puts on her dress.

The wind unfolds.
The wind is everything to them.

The Prediction

That night the moon drifted over the pond,
turning the water to milk, and under
the boughs of the trees, the blue trees,
a young woman walked, and for an instant

the future came to her:
rain falling on her husband's grave, rain falling
on the lawns of her children, her own mouth
filling with cold air, strangers moving into her house,

a man in her room writing a poem, the moon drifting into it,
a woman strolling under its trees, thinking of death,
thinking of him thinking of her, and the wind rising
and taking the moon and leaving the paper dark.

Breath

When you see them
tell them I am still here,

that I stand on one leg while the other one dreams,
that this is the only way,

that the lies I tell them are different
from the lies I tell myself,
that by being both here and beyond
I am becoming a horizon,

that as the sun rises and sets I know my place,
that breath is what saves me,
that even the forced syllables of decline are breath,
that if the body is a coffin it is also a closet of breath,

that breath is a mirror clouded by words,
that breath is all that survives the cry for help
as it enters the stranger's ear
and stays long after the word is gone,

that breath is the beginning again, that from it
all resistance falls away, as meaning falls
away from life, or darkness falls from light,
that breath is what I give them when I send my love.

The Remains

for Bill and Sandy Bailey

I empty myself of the names of others. I empty my pockets.
I empty my shoes and leave them beside the road.
At night I turn back the clocks;
I open the family album and look at myself as a boy.

What good does it do? The hours have done their job.
I say my own name. I say goodbye.
The words follow each other downwind.
I love my wife but send her away.

My parents rise out of their thrones
into the milky rooms of clouds. How can I sing?
Time tells me what I am. I change and I am the same.
I empty myself of my life and my life remains.

JOHN HAINES

Watching the Fire

Where are the Red Men?
They should be here. They saw the mound
of skulls glowing on the hearth.

For them the stone lamp flickered
and the drafty cave
was walled with visions.

The stories they told us were true,
we should have believed them:

a woman of brute form nurses her child—
wise eyes in a wrinkled skin,
forehead of horn—

he wears a necklace of fangs
and cries softly for flesh and blood.

The Lemmings

No one is pleased with himself
or with others.

No one squeaks gently
or touches a friendly nose.

In this darkness beneath
a calm whiteness
there are growls and scuffles;

the close smell of a neighbor
makes them all dream
of a brown river
swelling toward the sea.

In each small breast
the hated colony disintegrates.

The Cloud Factory

Mountains and cold places on the earth
are no man's garden:
there they make strange uses of rain.

Mist forms in the darkness among peaks
and valleys, like milk beaten thin.

It is rolled into bales,
shot full of damp stars
and pitched down the paths of glaciers.

The dawn wind carries these clouds
into cities and harbors,
to the sick bays and hospitals below.

And all this happens in an air of wrapped
sounds, the silence of bandages.

A magpie is watchman of the cloudworks;
he flies up and down,

the black and white holes of his plumage
disappearing into one another . . .

These are his wounds,
made whole in a cloud of grey feathers.

Foreboding

Something immense and lonely
divides the earth at evening.

For nine years I have watched
from an inner doorway:
as in a confused vision,
manlike figures approach, cover
their faces, and pass on,
heavy with iron and distance.

There is no sound but the wind
crossing the road, filling
the ruts with a dust as fine as chalk.

Like the closing of an inner door,
the day begins its dark
journey, across nine bridges
wrecked one by one.

CHARLES SIMIC

Dismantling the Silence

Take down its ears first
Carefully so they don't spill over.
With a sharp whistle slit its belly open.
If there are ashes in it, close your eyes
And blow them whichever way the wind is pointing.
If there's water, sleeping water,
Bring the root of a plant that hasn't drunk for a month.

When you reach the bones,
And you haven't got a pack of dogs with you,
And you haven't got a pine coffin
And a wagon pulled by oxen to make them rattle,
Slip them quickly under your skin,
Next time you pick up your sack,
You'll hear them setting your teeth on edge . . .

It is now completely dark.
Slowly and with patience
Feel its heart. You will need to haul
A heavy chest of drawers
Into its emptiness
To make it creak
On its wheel.

Fear

Fear passes from man to man
Unknowing,

As one leaf passes its shudder
To another.

All at once the whole tree is trembling
And there is no sign of the wind.

Last Supper

The teeth are first to come:
Two that were always left hungry.
The ears follow gloomily behind
Balancing themselves on stilts.

Then the eye arrives:
One millionth of an inch
Of pure longing.

The bones are already at the table:
White, delicate as maidenheads,
Their halos in place
Each hung by a meat hook.

The blood by now should be in the cups,
The hairs are making conversation.

There's also something trampled:
Tongue or tail it's hard to tell.
It snores under the table waiting for leftovers.

The one they are all waiting for
Is the last to sit down.
As he breaks this bandit's heart
Into thirteen morsels,
His throat swells:

He's a lunar rooster
Whose crow doesn't reach.

Invention of the Knife

Its blade imagined by the hanged man
in that split of a second as he glimpses
with raised eyes the rope for the last time

yields itself to his executioners
who then go home at daybreak
over the snow that makes no sound
to cut the bread fresh from the oven.

WILLIAM MATTHEWS

On Cape Cod a Child Is Stolen

Fog has sealed in the house
like a ship in a bottle.
All the people of the house
are dreaming of his future;
only the Puritans
and he aren't sleeping.
They watch him lie too long in bed,
the fog's moist nose at his ear.
Now the muzzle pokes his tiny mouth,
prying it open. They love him;
he's in danger; but it's too late.
His perfect body is still there
but clearly empty. The fog
rolls back to its own place
and the fishermen scrape back
from breakfast and go back to work.

Night Driving

You follow into their dark tips
those two skewed tunnels of light.
Ahead of you, they seem to meet.
When you blink, it is the future.

Sleep

Last cough,
lungcells six hours safe from cigarettes.
The testicles drone
in their hammocks
making sperm.
Glut and waste
and then the beach invasion,
people
everywhere, the earth in its regular
whirl slurring to silence
like a record at the onset
of a power failure.
I'm burning ferns to heat my house.
I am
the Population Bomb, no,
not a thing but a process:
fire: fire.

Ashes and seeds.
Now in my drowse I want to spend,
spend before the end.
Sleep with a snowflake,
wake with a wet wife.
This is the dream in which the word "pride"
appears as a comet.
Its tail is the whole language
you tried as a child to learn.

Difficult and flashy dreams!
But they're all
allegory, like that corny comet.
You can turn your head fast
and make the light smear,
and you wake to watch it
staining the windows, good
stunned morning, people
everywhere, all of us
unraveling, it's so good
to be alive.

❧

~~~~~~~~~~~~~~~~~~~~~~~~~~~~~~~~~~

JAMES HARRISON

~~~~~~~~~~~~~~~~~~~~~~~~~~~~~~~~~~

Cowgirl

The boots were on the couch and had
manure on their heels and tips.

The cowgirl with vermilion udders and ears
that tasted of cream pulled on her levis.

The saddle is not sore and the crotch with
its directionless brain is pounded by hammers.

Less like flowers than grease fittings women
win us to a life of holes, their negative space.

I don't know you and won't. You look at my hairline
while I work, conscious of history, in a bottomless lake.

Thighs that are indecently strong and have won the west,
I'll go back home where women are pliant as marshmallows.

VIII

from *Ghazals*

The color of a poppy and bruised, the sub-alpine green that
ascends the mountainside from where the eagle looked at
sheep.

Her sappy brain fleers, is part of the satin shirt (western) she
wears, chartreuse with red scarf. Poeet he says with two
"e's"!

The bull we frighten by waving our hats bellows, his pecker
lengthens touching the grass, he wheels, foam from the mouth.

How do we shoot those things that don't even know they're
animals
grazing and stalking in the high meadow: puma elk grizzly
deer.

When he pulled the trigger the deer bucked like a horse, spine
broken, grew pink in circles, became a lover kissing him
goodnight.

XXX

from *Ghazals*

I am walked on a leash by my dog and am water
only to be crossed by a bridge. Dog and bridge.

An ear not owned by a face, an egg without a yolk
and my mother without a rooster. Not to have been.

London has no bees and it is bee time. No hounds
in the orchard, no small craft warnings or sailing ships.

In how many poems through how many innocent branches
has the moon peeked without being round.

This song is for New York City who peeled me like
an apple, the fat off the lamb, raw and coreless.

V

from *Ghazals*

Yes yes yes it was the year of the tall ships
and the sea owned more and larger fish.

Antiquarians know that London's gutters were
pissed into openly and daggers worn by whores.

Smart's Geoffrey had distant relatives roaming
the docks hungry for garbage at dawn. Any garbage.

O Keats in Grassmere, walking, walking. Tom
is dead and this lover is loveless, loving.

Wordsworth stoops, laughs only once a month and then
in private, mourns a daughter on another shore.

But Keats' heart, Keats in Italy, Keats' heart
Keats how I love thee, I love thee John Keats.

MICHAEL BENEDIKT

Joy

How can I get through that innocence?
Jump through, and land in a damp swamp—?
No, I'd rather go bicycling

Around, and enjoy its transparent squalor
Starred with flowers so magnificent
Only the most rotted self-deception could impel them.

Another thing I like doing a lot
Is helping you across busy boulevards
With a specially enlargeable hand

Implying friendly aid at first,
Secondly, a growing degree of passion;
Then I inflate it and make it throb! I also enjoy

Watching you tremble in deserted underground tunnels
Your wonderful trembling, too, when we are side by side at
    midnight,
And kayaking in mid-Atlantic, alone.

DIANE WAKOSKI

The Night a Sailor Came to Me
in a Dream

At the point of shining feathers,
that moment when dawn
ran her finger along the knife-edge sky;
at the point when chickens come out of the living room ru⟮
to peck for corn and the grains like
old yellow eyes
roll as marbles across the floor;
at that sweet sprouting point when the seed of day
rests on your tongue,
and you haven't swallowed reality yet. Then,
then, yes, at that instant of shimmering new pine needles
came a dream, a blister from a new burn,
and you walked in,
old times,
no player piano or beer,
reality held my toes,
the silver ball of sleep was on my stomach,
the structure of dream
like a harness
lowered over my head, around me,
and I cannot remember what you said, though the harbor wa⟮
    foggy,
and your pea coat seemed to drip with moisture.

Thirty years of traveling this ocean.

Perhaps you told me
you were not
dead.

ERICA JONG

The Sheets

We used to meet
on this corner
in the same wind.
It fought us up the hill
to your house,
blew us in the door.
The elevator rose
on gusts of stale air
fed on ancient dinners.
Your room smelled
of roach spray and roses.

In those days
we went to bed with Marvell.
The wind ruffled sheets and pages,
spoke to us through walls.
For hours I used to lie
with my ear to your bare chest,
listening for the sea.

Now the wind is tearing
the building down.
The sheets are rising.

They billow through the air like sails.

White with your semen,
holding invisible prints
of the people we were,
the people we might have been,

they sail across the country
disguised as clouds.

Momentarily they snag
on the Rocky Mountains,
then rise
shredded into streamers.

Now they are bannering westward
over California
where your existence
is rumored.

Narcissus, Photographer

> . . . a frozen memory, like any photo
>   where nothing is missing, not even
>   and especially, nothingness . .
>
> —Julio Cortázar, "Blow Up"

Mirror-mad,
he photographed reflections:
sunstorms in puddles,
cities in canals,

double portraits framed
in sunglasses,
the fat phantoms who dance
on the flanks of cars.

Nothing caught his eye
unless it bent
or glistered
over something else.

He trapped clouds in bottles
the way kids

trap grasshoppers.
Then one misty day

he was stopped
by the windshield.
Behind him,
an avenue of trees,

before him,
the mirror of that scene.
He seemed to enter
what, in fact, he left.

NIKKI GIOVANNI

Poem for a Lady
Whose Voice I Like

so he said: you ain't got no talent
    if you didn't have a face
    you wouldn't be nobody

and she said: god created heaven and earth
    and all that's Black within them

so he said: you ain't really no hot shit
    they tell me plenty sisters
    take care better business than you

and she said: on the third day he made chitterlings
    and all good things to eat
    and said: "that's good"

so he said: if the white folks hadn't been under
         yo skirt and been giving you the big play
         you'd a had to come on uptown like everybody else

and she replied: then he took a big Black greasy rib
         from adam and said we will call this woeman and her
         name will be sapphire and she will divide into four parts
         that simone may sing a song

and he said: you pretty full of yourself ain't chu

so she replied: show me someone not full of herself
         and i'll show you a hungry person

The Geni in the Jar

(for Nina Simone)

take a note and spin it around spin it around don't
prick your finger
take a note and spin it around
on the Black loom on the Black loom
careful baby
don't prick your finger

take the air and weave the sky
around the Black loom around the Black loom
make the sky sing a Black song sing a blue song
sing my song make the sky sing a Black song
from the Black loom from the Black loom
careful baby
don't prick your finger

take the geni and put her in a jar
put her in a jar
wrap the sky around her
take the geni and put her in a jar
wrap the sky around her

listen to her sing
sing a Black song our Black song
from the Black loom
singing to me
from the Black loom
careful baby
don't prick your finger

HAROLD BOND

Him: The Roach

I know now. It has been him
after all, the same one I
have burned, flushed down my toilet,
crucified beneath my thumb

with equal redundancy.
I have never seen more than
one of him at one time. I
know now. I have watched him eye-

ball to eyeball. It has been
him: the roach. I have found him
in my pants, my hair, my soup.
I have lain in bed and seen

him tottering over me up-
side down on the ceiling. I
have tattooed him with pins and
buried him across town deep

under. And he has returned,
knock-kneed in an overplus
of paranoia. At night
I have risen from behind

locked doors only to know his
fullness. I have gone by touch
across this room, myopic,
and I have crushed out the face

of that one inkspot mismatch
on the floor, imagining
the horror of his silence,
his holiness, him: the roach.

SANDFORD LYNE

The Dog

The old, shade-baked dog bolted
off the porch,
the plowboys in a beat-up Chevy yelling
like wet flags, a towel
wrapped in the hubcap.   By the time
the dog caught up, he looked
like an enraged sud, running on stilts.
With a mercy that expects greater gore
the boys held off
the acid-gun from his eyes.
His snarling teeth
clinched in on the towel, took the bait,
took on
down his whole length the spin

of the tire, like
a woodstock on a lathe, his head
wrapped turban-fashion like a splayed
Saracen.   He felt every bone
snap and puncture
some inexpendable organ,
even for a dog.

When the towel worked loose
from the bloody
ornament of the smoking wheel, he did
not convulse or yelp,
or die.   But standing
kneedeep in his dropping guts, he took
the middle
of the road, and waited.
When the car turned around, came back
in a whine, he
planted himself like an iron
pick, met the grill
face to face, sent
his whole insides up the hood, the windshield, like
the world's biggest butterfly, blocked
the entire vision
of the onrushing earth, the shoulder,
ditch,
telephone pole, the
falling sky

in the kingdom of dog.

Notes on the Poets

JAMES AGEE (1910–1955), born in Knoxville, Tennessee. Though best known as a film critic and novelist (*The Morning Watch* and *A Death in the Family*), Agee began his career with the publication of *Permit Me Voyage*, a book of poems which won the Yale Younger Poets Award in 1934, and continued writing poetry until his death. His lyrical prose commentaries on Walker Evans' photographs of sharecroppers in the South, *Let Us Now Praise Famous Men*, appeared in 1941. Works include: *Collected Poems* (Houghton Mifflin, 1968).

KINGSLEY AMIS (1922–   ), born in London. The mordant wit of Amis' novels (*Lucky Jim* and *Take a Girl Like You* among others) distinguishes his poetry as well. He is a critic and anthologist of science fiction, having compiled several volumes of stories (with Robert Conquest) and written one of the best studies of that genre (*New Maps of Hell: A Survey of Science-Fiction*, 1960). Works include: *A Case of Samples* (Gollancz, 1957); *A Look Round the Estate* (Jonathan Cape, 1967).

A. R. AMMONS (1926–   ), born in Whiteville, North Carolina. Ammons was the principal of an elementary school in his native state at the age of 26, then worked as an executive in a glass factory, and at present teaches at Cornell University. Works include: *Selected Poems* (Cornell University Press, 1968); *Briefings* (W. W. Norton, 1971).

JOHN ASHBERY (1927–   ), born in Rochester, New York. Ashbery has written several plays and novels as well as poetry. At one time the art critic for the Paris *Tribune*, he is at present executive editor of *Art News*. Ashbery is associated, along with James Schuyler, Kenneth Koch and Frank O'Hara, with the "New York School." Works include: *Rivers and Mountains* (Holt, Rinehart & Winston, 1966); *The Double Dream of Spring* (E. P. Dutton, 1970); *Three Poems* (Viking, 1972).

W. H. AUDEN (1907–1973), born in York, England. After residing in the United States as a citizen since 1939, Auden returned to England in 1972 to make his home at Oxford. Works include: *Collected Shorter Poems* (Random House, 1967); *Collected Longer Poems* (Random House, 1969); *About the House* (Random House, 1965); *City Without Walls* (Random House, 1969).

RONALDO AZEREDO (1937–   ), born in Rio de Janeiro, Brazil. A member of the Noigandre Group of Concrete poets, Azeredo has published his poems in the Brazilian review *Invençao* and in magazines and anthologies throughout the world. He came to Concrete poetry directly, without ever having written traditional poems.

SAMUEL BECKETT (1906–   ), born in Dublin. Though Beckett's poems are comparatively little known, they are equal in their visionary power and multifaceted wit to his novels and plays. Several of his poems were published during the thirties in Eugene Jolas' *transition*; and others, written in French, appeared in Paris literary reviews. Works include: *Poems in English* (Grove, 1961).

MICHAEL BENEDIKT (1937–   ), born in New York City. The poet has published art criticism in *Art News* and *Art International*. Works include: *The Body* (Wesleyan University Press, 1968); *Sky* (Wesleyan University Press, 1970); *Mole Notes* (Wesleyan University Press, 1971).

JOHN BERRYMAN (1914–1972), born in McAlester, Oklahoma. Berryman was one of the most esteemed of the generation of poets that included Delmore Schwartz, Randall Jarrell, Theodore Roethke and Robert Lowell. His mercurial style continued to change up to the time of his death by suicide in

ᴇ winter of 1972. Berryman was also a critic and the author
ᶠ a biography of Stephen Crane. Works include: *Homage to
ᴍistress Bradstreet* (Farrar, Straus & Cudahy, 1956); *77
ᴅream Songs* (Farrar, Straus & Giroux, 1964); *Berryman's
ᴄonnets* (Farrar, Straus & Giroux, 1967); *Short Poems* (Far-
ᴀr, Straus & Giroux, 1967); *His Toy, His Dream, His Rest*
ᶠarrar, Straus & Giroux, 1969).

ᴏHN BETJEMAN (1906–   ), born in London. The poet,
ᴋnighted by the Queen in 1969, is one of the most popular
ᴀnd successful authors of "light verse" in England since Win-
ᴀrop Mackworth Praed. Works include: *Collected Poems*
ᴊohn Murray, 1958).

ᴇLIZABETH BISHOP (1911–   ), born in Worcester,
ᴍassachusetts. The elegant wit and formal poise of her poetry
ᴇstablished her reputation with the appearance of her first
ᴠolume in the forties. She lives half the year in Brazil. Works
ᴉnclude: *Complete Poems* (Farrar, Straus & Giroux, 1970).

ᴿOBERT BLY (1926–   ), born in Madison, Minnesota.
ᴮly has edited the influential literary journal *The Sixties* (now
ᴛhe Seventies); is a translator of Scandinavian and Spanish
ᴘoetry; and has organized many poetry readings in opposition
ᴛo the war in Vietnam. Works include: *Silence in the Snowy
ᶠields* (Wesleyan University Press, 1962); *The Light Around
ᴛhe Body* (Harper & Row, 1967).

ᴴAROLD BOND (1939–   ), born in Boston, Massachu-
ᴇtts. A selection of his poems appeared in *The Young Amer-
ᴉcan Poets,* edited by Paul Carroll (Follett, 1968).

ᴿICHARD BRAUTIGAN (1935–   ), born in the Pacific
ᴺorthwest. The fey and alembicated wit of Brautigan's more
ᶠamous novels (*Trout Fishing in America, A Confederate
ᴳeneral from Big Sur, The Abortion: An Historical Romance
1966)* is also distilled by his poetry. Works include: *The Pill
ᴠersus the Springhill Mine Disaster* (Delta, 1968); *Rommel
ᴅrives on Deep into Egypt* (Dell, 1970).

CHARLES BUKOWSKI (1920–   ), born in Andermach, Germany. The poet was taken to the United States at the age of two and grew up on the West Coast. Generally associated with the "Beat" movement, he writes a weekly column for the underground paper *Open City,* published in California, called "Notes of a Dirty Old Man." Works include: *It Catches My Heart in Its Hands* (Loujon Press, 1963); *Crucifix in a Death-hand* (Lyle Stuart, 1965).

BASIL BUNTING (1900–   ), born in Northumbria, England. In 1938 Ezra Pound dedicated his *Guide to Kulchur* to both Basil Bunting and Louis Zukovsky as companion "strugglers in the desert"; but since the publication of Bunting's *Briggflatts* in 1966, he has been recognized widely as one of the chief poets of his generation. Works include: *Collected Poems* (Fulcrum Press, 1968).

JOSEPH CERAVOLO (1934–   ), born in New York City. Ceravolo's poetic style gravitates somewhat toward the sophisticated pidgin of Gertrude Stein, but moves in an eccentric orbit of its own. He is generally associated with the "New York School" of poets. Works include: *Wild Flowers Out of Gas* (Tibor de Nagy, 1967); *Spring in This World of Poor Mutts* (Columbia University Press, 1968).

GREGORY CORSO (1930–   ), born in New York City. A street waif reared in reform schools and educated in the bistros of Greenwich Village, Corso rose by pluck, grit and chutzpah like an Horatio Alger hero to become, not a millionaire, but one of the best known poets of the "Beat" generation. Works include: *Gasoline* (City Lights Books, 1958); *The Happy Birthday of Death* (New Directions, 1959); *Long Live Man* (New Directions, 1962); *Selected Poems* (Eyre & Spottiswoode, 1962).

ROBERT CREELEY (1926–   ), born in Arlington, Massachusetts. The poet served with the American Field Service in Burma during World War II. One of the most influential members of the "Black Mountain School," Creeley edited the *Black Mountain Review* while teaching at that college. Works include: *For Love* (Scribner's, 1962); *Words* (Scribner's, 1967); *Pieces* (Scribner's, 1969).

e. e. cummings (1894–1962), born in Cambridge, Massachusetts. The poet-painter of Patchin Place in Greenwich Village continues to be one of the most widely read and influential writers of his generation, an honored ancestor of both Concrete and Beat. Works include: *Poems 1923–1954* (Harcourt Brace & World, 1958); *95 Poems* (Harcourt Brace & World, 1958).

J. V. CUNNINGHAM (1911–   ), born in Maryland. Cunningham spent his boyhood years in Montana, which he considers his heartland. A student of Yvor Winters at Stanford University in California, he began writing poetry and criticism under his influence, but has since achieved his own distinctive and powerful style. Works include: *The Exclusions of a Rhyme* (Swallow Press, 1960); *To What Strangers, What Welcome* (Swallow Press, 1964).

DONALD DAVIE (1922–   ), born in Yorkshire, England. Davie is as well known for his criticism *(Articulate Energy* and *Ezra Pound: Poet as Sculptor)* as for his finely wrought lyric poetry. He has read his poems and lectured widely both in the United States and in England. Works include: *A Sequence for Francis Parkman* (Marvell Press, 1961); *Events & Wisdoms* (Routledge, 1964); *Essex Poems* (Routledge, 1969).

WALTER DE LA MARE (1873–1956), born in Kent, England. De La Mare was one of the chief exemplars of the pre-World War I Georgian school, but as a poet of Ariel-like evanescence (as W. H. Auden described him) and delicacy of touch, his true ancestry may be found in the lyricists of Elizabethan England. He is famous also as a novelist *(Memoirs of a Midget)* and an anthologist *(Come Hither)*. Works include: *Collected Poems* (Holt, Rinehart and Winston, 1941).

JAMES DICKEY (1923–   ), born in Atlanta, Georgia. A novelist *(Deliverance)* and critic *(Babel to Byzantium)* as well as a poet, Dickey has served as Consultant in Poetry to the Library of Congress and currently teaches at the University of South Carolina. Works include: *Poems 1957–1967* (Wesleyan University Press, 1967).

REINHARD DÖHL (1934–   ), born in Wattenscheid, Germany. Döhl currently lives in Stuttgart. Works include: *prosa zum beispiel* (1965); *4 texte* (1965); *es anna* (1966).

ALAN DUGAN (1923–   ), born in Brooklyn, New York. Dugan's first book, *Poems*, won both the National Book Award and the Pulitzer Prize in 1962. He has lectured and read his poetry at college campuses throughout the United States. Works include: *Collected Poems* (Yale University Press, 1969).

ROBERT DUNCAN (1919–   ), born in Oakland, California. Associated since the late forties with the "Black Mountain School." Works include: *The Opening of the Field* (Grove, 1960); *Roots and Branches* (New Directions, 1964); *Bending the Bow* (New Directions, 1968); *The Years as Catches: First Poems 1939–1946* (Oyez Press, 1965); *Epilogos* (Black Sparrow Press, 1967).

RUSSELL EDSON (1928-   ), born in New York City. Edson's shamanistic prose-poems, in which the ghosts that haunt the surreal and violent world of American comic strips have been released from their boxes and set at large, are somewhat reminiscent of the work of Edward Lear, Christian von Morganstern and, especially, Henry Michaux. His original line drawings for his poems are in the same spirit. Works include: *The Very Thing That Happens* (New Directions, 1964).

LARRY EIGNER (1927–   ), born in Swampscott, Massachusetts. Eigner has been associated with the "Black Mountain School" of poets since the early fifties. Works include: *The–/Towards Autumn* (Black Sparrow Press, 1967); *Another Time in Fragments* (Fulcrum Press, 1967).

D. J. ENRIGHT (1920–   ), born in Leamington, Warwickshire, England. The poet spent many years after World War II in the Far East, where he was at one time a professor of English literature at the University of Singapore. He is currently the co-editor of the magazine *Encounter* in London. Works include: *Unlawful Assembly* (Chatto & Windus, 1968); *The Typewriter Revolution & Other Poems* (Library Press, 1971).

KENNETH FEARING (1902–1961), born in Oak Park, Illinois. Fearing's metropolitan style and sensibility, though formed in the depression years of the thirties, make him almost a contemporary. Works include: *New and Selected Poems* (Indiana University Press, 1956).

ALVIN FEINMAN (1930–   ), born in New York City. The poet has been an instructor in philosophy at Yale University, and currently teaches at Bennington. He has written one book of poems: *Preambles and Other Poems* (Oxford University Press, 1964).

EDWARD FIELD (1924–   ), born in New York City. The poet won the 1962 Lamont Poetry Award for his first volume, *Stand Up, Friend, with Me*. Works include: *Stand Up, Friend, with Me* (Grove, 1963); *Variety Photoplays* (Grove, 1967).

IAN HAMILTON FINLAY (1925–   ), born in Scotland. Finlay is undoubtedly the most inventive as well as prolific of the Concrete poets in England. He is the founder of the Wild Hawthorn Press, in Lanarkshire, Scotland, which publishes his poems and poem-prints, pamphlets, etc. Works include: *The Dancers Inherit the Party* (1959); *Telegrams from My Windmill* (1964).

FORD MADOX FORD (Ford Madox Hueffer, 1873–1939), born in London. One of the most creative and influential forces in modern literature, Ford assisted the young Ezra Pound as well as many other authors with aid and critical advice. He is best known for his novels *Parade's*

End and *The Good Soldier*, but his poems, published toward
the end of his life, are also distinguished. Works include:
Buckshee (Pym-Randall Press, 1966).

ALLEN GINSBERG (1926–   ), born in Newark, New
Jersey. With the publication of *Howl* in 1956, as much a
social as a literary phenomenon, Ginsberg became the poetic
voice of the Beat movement in the United States. Works
include: *Howl and Other Poems* (City Lights Books, 1956);
Kaddish and Other Poems (City Lights Books, 1961); *Reality
Sandwiches* (City Lights Books, 1963); *Planet News* (City
Lights Books, 1968).

NIKKI GIOVANNI (1943–   ), born in Knoxville, Tennessee. The two most fateful events in her life, the poet
declared a few years ago, were that she "was expelled from
Fiske and was once in love." She is the author of a book of
memoirs, *Gemini*, published by Bobbs-Merrill in 1972, and
has read her poems widely at college campuses and on television. Works include: *Black Feeling* (Broadside Press, 1968).

EUGEN GOMRINGER (1924–   ), born in Bolivia. The
founder of Concrete poetry as an international movement,
along with Decio Pignatari of Brazil, Gomringer has produced
numerous volumes of his own poems, called by him "constellations," as well as published the poems of others. He established the Eugen Gomringer Press in Frauenfeld, Switzerland,
where he makes his home. Works include: *Die Konstella-
tionem* (Gomringer Press, 1964); *Manifeste und Darstellun-
gen der Konkreten Poesie* (Gallerie Press, 1966).

SAMUEL GREENBERG (1893–1917), born in Russia.
Greenberg died in a tuberculosis sanitarium at the age of 24,
leaving behind a mass of unpublished poems scribbled in
nickel notebooks. When these by chance came to the attention of Hart Crane, he immediately recognized their visionary
power and incorporated several of Greenberg's lines and
images into his own work. Works include: *Poems*, edited by
Harold Holden and Jack McMannis (Holt, 1947).

THOM GUNN (1929–   ), born in Gravesend, England. Gunn began his career as a member of "The Movement" group of poets in England after World War II, which included Donald Davie and Philip Larkin among others. He has lived in the United States for many years. Works include: *Fighting Terms* (Faber & Faber, 1962); *Positives* (Faber & Faber, 1966); *Touch* (Faber & Faber, 1967).

JOHN HAINES (1924–   ), born in Norfolk, Virginia. After fifteen years as a homesteader in northern Alaska, Haines moved in 1969 to the California coast. Works include: *Winter News* (Wesleyan, 1966); *The Stone Harp* (Wesleyan, 1971).

JIM HARRISON (1937–   ), born in Michigan. The poet makes his home on a farm in northern Michigan. He was formerly a co-editor of the magazine *Sumac* and poetry editor of the *Nation*. Works include: *Plain Song* (Norton, 1965); *Locations* (Norton, 1968); *Outlyer and Ghazals* (Simon & Schuster, 1971).

ANTHONY HECHT (1922–   ), born in New York City. The poet has taught at several colleges in the United States, and is currently on the faculty of the University of Rochester. Works include: *A Summoning of Stones* (Macmillan, 1954); *The Hard Hours* (Atheneum, 1967).

ERNEST HEMINGWAY (1899–1961), born in Oak Park, Illinois. Hemingway wrote a number of poems, under the influence of Gertrude Stein and Ezra Pound, between courses at the Moveable Feast during the twenties in Paris. Most of them were published in various avant-garde literary magazines, including *Der Querschmitt*, *The Little Review* and *The Double Dealer*. Works include: *Collected Poems* (Pirated Edition, San Francisco, 1960).

ANSELM HOLLO (1934–   ), born in Helsinki, Finland. A translator of Russian, Finnish, French and German poetry, as well as the author of more than fourteen volumes of his own poetry, Hollo currently is teaching in the United States. Works include: *The Coherences* (Trigram Press, 1968).

TED HUGHES (1930–   ), born in Yorkshire, England. Hughes served in the R.A.F. as a ground wireless operator after the war, and has taught and read widely in the United States. He was married to Sylvia Plath. Works include: *The Hawk in the Rain* (Faber & Faber, 1958); *Lupercal* (Faber & Faber, 1960); *Crow* (Harper & Row, 1971).

RANDALL JARRELL (1914–1965), born in Nashville, Tennessee. Jarrell is equally well known for his criticism—"the last of the great poet-critics," Robert Lowell once called him—which helped set the literary tone of the forties and fifties. Works include: *The Complete Poems* (Farrar, Straus & Giroux, 1969).

RONALD JOHNSON (1935–   ), born in Ashland, Kansas. Ronald Johnson, so he states, was educated at Columbia and re-educated at the Cedar Bar in Greenwich Village. Works include: *A Line of Poetry, A Row of Trees* (Jargon Press, 1964); *Gerse/Goose/Rose* (University of Indiana Press, 1966); *The Book of the Green Man* (Norton, 1967).

DAVID JONES (1895–   ), born in Wales. Jones' two most important books emerged out of the trauma of war: *In Parenthesis,* based on his experiences as a member of the Royal Welsh Fusiliers in World War I, and *The Anathemata,* which was begun during World War II. Jones is a convert to the Catholic faith. Works include: *In Parenthesis* (Viking, 1961); *The Anathemata* (Viking, 1965); *The Tribune's Visitation* (Fulcrum Press, 1969).

LEROI JONES (1934–   ), born in Newark, New Jersey. As a poet living on New York's East Side, LeRoi Jones was an editor of *Yugen* magazine and of the Totem Press; now, having changed his name to Imamu Amiri Baraka, he is a political activist in his hometown of Newark. Works include: *Preface to a Twenty Volume Suicide Note* (Totem Press, 1961); *The Dead Lecturer* (Grove, 1964).

ERICA JONG (1942–   ), born in New York City. The poet has read her work on television as well as on college campuses across the United States. Works include: *Fruits and Vegetables* (Holt, Rinehart and Winston, 1971).

WELDON KEES (1914–1955), born in Nebraska. Kees was a film critic, jazz composer, short-story writer and painter as well as poet. He died under mysterious circumstances: some say he jumped from the Golden Gate Bridge in San Francisco, others say that he merely disappeared and is still living somewhere in South America. His poetry has continued to grow in importance. Works include: *Collected Poems* (Stonewall Press, 1960).

ROBERT KELLY (1935–   ), born in Brooklyn, New York. A founder and editor of *Chelsea Review* and *Trober,* Kelly also runs the Matter Press. He was co-editor of the anthology *A Controversy of Poets* (Doubleday, 1965). Works include: *A Joining* (Black Sparrow Press, 1967); *Finding the Measure* (Black Sparrow Press, 1968).

JACK KEROUAC (1922–1969), born in Lowell, Massachusetts. Though primarily known for his novels *(On the Road* and *The Dharma Bums),* which became the chief manifestos of the Beat movement, Kerouac was also an improvisatory poet. As he wrote: "I want to be considered a jazz poet blowing a long blues in an afternoon jam session on Sunday." Works include: *Mexico City Blues* (Grove, 1959); *The Scripture of the Golden Eternity* (Totem Press, 1960).

GALWAY KINNELL (1927–   ), born in Providence, Rhode Island. Kinnell has published translations of poetry by Yvan Goll, Yves Bonnefoy and François Villon. Works include: *Body Rags* (Houghton Mifflin, 1968); *The Book of Nightmares* (Houghton Mifflin, 1971).

THOMAS KINSELLA (1928–   ), born in Dublin, Ireland. A translator of poetry from the Gaelic, Kinsella served as a member of the Irish Civil Service until 1965. After his resignation, he emigrated to the United States, where he has lectured and read his poetry at college campuses throughout the country. Works include: *Another September* (Dolmen Press, 1958); *Selected Poems* (Dolmen Press, 1964).

BILL KNOTT (1940–   ), born in Chicago, Illinois. Of himself the author has written, "Bill Knott (1940–1966) is a virgin and a suicide." Reincarnated as "Saint Geraud," he now makes his home in New York and at the MacDowell Colony in New Hampshire. Works include: *The Naomi Poems: Corpse and Beans* (Follett, 1958).

KENNETH KOCH (1925–   ), born in Cincinnati, Ohio. One of the founders of the "New York School" of poets from the Midwest and New England, educated at Harvard, Koch has written several verse plays for the theater (*Bertha and Other Plays*, 1966) and published a book based on his experience in teaching children how to write poetry (*Wishes, Lies and Dreams*, 1971). He currently teaches at Columbia University, and for several years has been editor of the magazine *Locus Solus*. Works include: *Ko, or A Season on Earth* (Grove, 1960); *Thank You and Other Poems* (Grove, 1962); *The Pleasures of Peace and Other Poems* (Grove, 1969).

PHILIP LAMANTIA (1927–   ), born in San Francisco, California. An early American surrealist and editor of the magazine *View*, Lamantia broke with the movement in 1946 and went his own way across the "great Gromboolian plain" of the United States like Edward Lear's Dong with the Luminous Nose. Works include: *Selected Poems* (City Lights Books, 1967).

PHILIP LARKIN (1922–   ), born in England. With the poets Donald Davie and Thom Gunn, Larkin was associated after World War II in the movement capitalized as "The Movement," a poetic counterpart to "The Angry Young Men" in the theater. Works include: *The North Ship* (Marvell Press, 1945); *The Less Deceived* (Marvell Press, 1955); *The Whitsun Weddings* (Marvell Press, 1964).

DENISE LEVERTOV (1923–   ), born in London. The poet came to the United States after World War II and has since made her home here. Generally associated with the "Black Mountain School" of poets, she has read her poems widely at colleges throughout the country. Works include: *The Jacob's Ladder* (New Directions, 1961); *O Taste and See* (New Directions, 1964); *Sorrow Dance* (New Directions, 1967); *A Tree Telling of Orpheus* (Black Sparrow Press, 1968).

CHRISTOPHER LOGUE (1926–   ), born in London. Logue's translations from the classics, including "free" adaptations of passages from Homer's *Iliad,* have received wide critical acclaim. He has also written several plays for the Royal Court Theater in London, and has turned his hand at poster-poems and jazz lyrics. Since 1962 he has done a biweekly column for the English review *Private Eye.* Works include: *New Numbers* (Knopf, 1970).

ROBERT LOWELL (1917–   ), born in Boston, Massachusetts. Lowell has won more praises and prizes than any poet of his generation. Works include: *Lord Weary's Castle* (Harcourt Brace, 1946); *Life Studies* (Farrar, Straus & Cudahy, 1959); *For the Union Dead* (Farrar, Straus & Giroux, 1964); *Near the Ocean* (Farrar, Straus & Giroux, 1967); *Notebooks* (Farrar, Straus & Giroux, 1969).

MINA LOY (1882–1966), born in London. She was early associated with the Objectivist movement in poetry centered around Ezra Pound in Europe and William Carlos Williams and Louis Zukovsky in the United States. Her work, out of print for years, was revived for a younger generation, to whom she had become merely a name, after being republished by Jonathan Williams' Jargon Press. Works include: *Lunar Baedeker and Time-Tables* (Jargon Press, 1958).

SANDFORD LYNE (1945–   ), born in Kendallville, Indiana. He has published poetry in various literary magazines, and was represented in the anthology *Quickly Aging Here,* edited by Geof Hewitt (Doubleday Anchor, 1969).

GEORGE MacBETH (1932–   ), born in Scotland. Mac
Beth has edited several anthologies of poetry and worked f
the B.B.C. in England as a producer of "talk" shows. Work
include: *The Colour of Blood* (Macmillan, 1967); *The Nig*
of Stones (Macmillan, 1968); *The Burning Cone* (Macmilla
1970).

HUGH MacDIARMID (Christopher Grieve, 1892–
born in Langholme, Scotland. A Scottish nationalist and poli
ical radical in the tradition of Robert Burns, MacDiarm
has written translations of Scottish poetry, an autobiograph
fiction, etc., as well as several volumes of verse. Works i
clude: *Collected Poems* (Macmillan, 1962).

LOUIS MacNEICE (1907–1963), born in Belfast, Irelan
Along with W. H. Auden, C. Day Lewis and Stephen Spende
MacNeice emerged as a poet during the "Wasteland" thirti
in England. He was a classical scholar and translator as we
as the author of a famous travel book, *Letters from Icelan*
in collaboration with W. H. Auden. Works include: *Collecte*
Poems (Faber & Faber, 1966).

MICHAEL McCLURE (1932–   ), born in the Midwes
One of the most original and unventriloquized of the poets
the generation vaguely associated with the Beat movemen
McClure currently makes his home in San Francisco. Work
include: *Dark Brown* (Auerhahn, 1967); *Little Odes and th*
Raptors (Black Sparrow Press, 1969).

WILLIAM MATTHEWS (1942–   ), born in Cincinna
Ohio. Mathews is co-editor of the magazine *Lillabulero* an
teaches at Cornell University. Works include: *Ruining t*
New Road (Random House, 1970).

SAMUEL MENASHE (1925–   ), born in New York Cit
Menashe's first book of poetry, *The Many Named Belov*
(Gollancz, 1961), was published in England, where it w
wide acclaim. Works include: *No Jerusalem But This* (Oct
ber House, 1971).

JAMES MERRILL (1926–   ), born in New York City. Merrill has written several novels *(The Seraglio* and *The Diblos Notebook)* and plays *(The Immortal Husband* and *The Bait)* as well as poetry, for which he received the National Book Award in 1967. Works include: *Water Street* (Atheneum, 1962); *Nights and Days* (Atheneum, 1966); *The Fire Screen* (Atheneum, 1969).

W. S. MERWIN (1927–   ), born in New York City. A gifted translator of French, Spanish and Portuguese poetry, Merwin lived in Europe for many years before returning to the United States. His poetic style, rooted in a profoundly personal yet universal source of metaphor, has continued to exfoliate over the years. Works include: *The Drunk in the Furnace* (Macmillan, 1960); *The Moving Target* (Atheneum, 1963); *The Lice* (Atheneum, 1967); *The Carrier of Ladders* (Atheneum, 1970).

CHRISTOPHER MIDDLETON (1923–   ), born in Cornwall, England. Middleton is well known as a translator of modern German poetry, especially the work of Gottfried Benn, and has also written libretti for operas. He has taught widely in the United States and in England. Works include: *Nonsequences* (W. W. Norton, 1965); *Our Flowers and Nice Bones* (Fulcrum, 1969).

HOWARD MOSS (1922–   ), born in New York City. The poet has written several plays for the theater, including *The Palace at 4 A.M.* and *The Oedipus Mah-Jongg Scandal,* and has served as poetry editor for many years at *The New Yorker* magazine. He was awarded the National Book Award for 1972. Works include: *Selected Poems* (Atheneum, 1971).

EDWIN MUIR (1887–1958), born in the Orkneys, Scotland. Muir was an editor and translator, critic, author of a remarkable autobiography *(The Story and the Fable),* and, of course, a rare poet. Works include: *Collected Poems* (Grove, 1953).

HOWARD NEMEROV (1920–   ), born in New York City. The poet has lectured and read his poems widely in colleges throughout the United States. Works include: *New and Selected Poems* (University of Chicago Press, 1960); *The Blue Swallow* (University of Chicago Press, 1967).

SEIICHI NIIKUNI (1925–   ), born in Japan. Niikuni has won an international reputation as one of the purest and most inventive of the Japanese Concrete poets. Works include: *Zero On* (1963); *Poèmes franco-japonais* (with Pierre Garnier, Editions André Silvaire, 1966).

VLADISLAV NOVÁK (1925–   ), born in Turnov, Czechoslovakia. A poet and painter and self-described "unorthodox surrealist," Novák has exhibited his work widely throughout Western Europe. A selection of his experimental writings from 1959 to 1964 was published in Prague in 1966 under the title *Pacta Jacksonn Pollookovi (Homage to Jackson Pollock).*

FRANK O'HARA (1926–1966), born in Baltimore, Maryland. At the time of his death in the summer of 1966, when he was struck by a dune buggy on the beach at Fire Island, O'Hara, one of the founders of the "New York School," had not yet fully realized his gifts as a poet. He was a curator of paintings at the Museum of Modern Art in New York, and arranged many of its exhibitions, notably that of Jackson Pollock, for shows here and abroad. Works include: *Meditations in an Emergency* (Grove, 1957); *Lunch Poems* (City Lights Books, 1964); *In Memory of My Feelings* (Museum of Modern Art, 1967).

CHARLES OLSON (1910–1970), born in Worcester, Massachusetts. Critic, teacher and poet, Olson was a founder of the "Black Mountain School" along with Robert Creeley and Robert Duncan. Works include: *The Maximus Poems* (Jargon Press, 1960); *The Distances* (Grove Press, 1961); *Mayan Letters,* edited by Robert Creeley (Owers Press, Mallorca, 1953); *Call Me Ishmael* (City Lights Books, 1966).

ELDER OLSON (1909–   ), born in Chicago, Illinois. A noted critic and scholar as well as a poet, Olson has maintained the integrity of his own classically austere and lucent style throughout the many changes in literary fashion. Works include: *Plays and Poems: 1948–1958* (University of Chicago Press, 1959).

GEORGE OPPEN (1908–   ), born in New Rochelle, New York. Oppen was early associated with the Objectivist movement in the United States, and his first book, *Discrete Series*, published in 1934, was prefaced by Ezra Pound. He was awarded a Pulitzer Prize for poetry in 1969. Works include: *The Materials* (New Directions, 1962); *This In Which* (New Directions, 1965); *Of Being Numerous* (New Directions, 1968).

KENNETH PATCHEN (1911–1972), born in Ohio. A spinal illness from which he suffered throughout his life kept the poet immobilized, but his buoyant and irrepressible spirit enabled him to produce numerous books of poems, picture-poems (for he was an excellent draftsman as well), novels, scenarios, etc. His reputation was at its highest when he died. Works include: *Collected Poems* (New Directions, 1968).

DÉCIO PIGNATARI (1927–   ), born in Sao Paulo, Brazil. One of the founders of the movement of Concrete poetry, Pignatari is director of the review *Invençao* in Brazil. He joined with Augusto and Haraldo de Campos in 1952 to form the Noigandres Group of Concrete poets. He has published translations of Pound's *Cantos* into Portuguese. Works include: *Teoria da Poesia Concreta* (1965).

SYLVIA PLATH (1932–1963), born in Boston, Massachusetts. Since her death by her own hand and the republication of her autobiographical novels *(The Colossus* and *The Bell Jar)*, Sylvia Plath has become an almost legendary figure. Works include: *The Colossus and Other Poems* (Knopf, 1962); *Ariel* (Harper & Row, 1966); *Crossing the Water* (Harper & Row, 1971.)

EZRA POUND (1885–1972), born in Idaho. The most poly-semous and polyphiloprogenitive poet of his age, who "gathered from the air a live tradition," Pound was still an embattled figure when he died at the age of 87 in Venice on Nov. 1, 1972. Works include: *Personae* (New Directions, 1949); *The Cantos—1–95* (New Directions, 1963); *Thrones—Cantos 96–109* (New Directions, 1959); *Drafts & Fragments of Cantos 110–117* (New Directions, 1968); *The Translations of Ezra Pound* (New Directions, 1963).

F. T. PRINCE (1912–   ), born in Kimberley, South Africa. Prince was one of the most powerful and innovative poets to appear in England during the late thirties. He has lectured widely in English universities and is now a teacher at the University of Southampton. Works include: *Poems* (Faber & Faber, 1938); *Soldiers Bathing and Other Poems* (Fortune Press, 1954); *The Doors of Stone* (Faber & Faber, 1963); *Memoirs in Oxford* (Fulcrum, 1963).

KENNETH REXROTH (1905–   ), born in Indiana. A painter and essayist as well as a poet, Rexroth has been part of the San Francisco scene since World War II. Works include: *The Collected Shorter Poems* (New Directions, 1966); *The Collected Longer Poems* (New Directions, 1968).

CHARLES REZNIKOFF (1894–   ), born in Brooklyn, New York. Reznikoff was one of the most original of the poets associated with the "Objectivist School" of poetry in the twenties and thirties. Works include: *In Memoriam: 1933* (The Objectivist Press, 1934); *Jerusalem the Golden* (The Objectivist Press, 1934); *By the Waters of Manhattan* (New Directions, 1962); *Testimony: the United States, 1885–1890* (New Directions, 1965).

THEODORE ROETHKE (1908–1963), born in Saginaw, Michigan. Roethke's hard-won style has altered the poetic conventions of the present age. Works include: *Collected Poems* (Doubleday, 1966).

ARAM SAROYAN (1943–   ), born in New York City. The son of the playwright and short-story writer William Saroyan, Aram Saroyan is one of the leading exponents of

Concrete poetry in the United States. Works include: *Pages* (Random House, 1969); *Cloth* (Big Table, 1971).

JAMES SCHUYLER (1923–   ), born in Chicago, Illinois. A curator of paintings at the Museum of Modern Art, Schuyler is generally associated with the "New York School" of poets. He collaborated with John Ashbery to write a novel called *A Nest of Ninnies,* published in 1969 by E. P. Dutton. Works include: *Freely Espousing* (Paris Review-Doubleday, 1969).

DELMORE SCHWARTZ (1913–1966), born in Brooklyn, New York. A critic and writer of short stories as well as a poet, Schwartz served as an editor of *Partisan Review* during the heyday of that magazine in the late forties and fifties. Works include: *Selected Poems* (New Directions, 1957); *Successful Love* (Corinth, 1961); *Summer Knowledge* (New Directions, 1959).

CHARLES SIMIC (1938–   ), born in Yugoslavia. Simic has published numerous translations of French, Russian, and Yugoslav poetry. Works include: *What the Grass Says* (Kayak Press, 1967); *Somewhere Among Us a Stone Is Taking Notes* (Kayak Press, 1969); *Dismantling the Silence* (George Braziller, 1971).

LOUIS SIMPSON (1923–   ), born in Jamaica, British West Indies. The poet served as an infantryman in Europe during World War II, an experience which provided him with many of the themes of his early work. His style has continued to evolve in depth and complexity. Works include: *Selected Poems* (Harcourt Brace & World, 1965); *Adventures of the Letter I* (Harper & Row, 1971).

STEVIE SMITH (Florence Margaret Smith, 1902–1970), born in Yorkshire, England. The poet not only illustrated her own books but read and sang her poems, based on plainsong and folk music, at festivals in England. What Robert Lowell once called her "unique and cheerfully gruesome voice" was tuned by a superb lyric skill that made her one of the most highly regarded stylists of her time. Works include: *Selected Poems* (New Directions, 1964).

W. D. SNODGRASS (1926–   ), born in Beaver Falls, Pennsylvania. The poet's first collection, *Heart's Needle*, won the Pulitzer Prize in 1960. Works include: *Heart's Needle* (Harper & Row, 1959); *After Experience* (Harper & Row, 1968).

GARY SNYDER (1930–   ), born in San Francisco, California. Snyder has lived many years in Japan and India as a student of Zen. Works include: *Myths and Texts* (Totem Press, 1960); *The Back Country* (New Directions, 1967).

MARY ELLEN SOLT (1920–   ), born in Gilmore City, Iowa. After a visit to Ian Hamilton Finlay in Scotland in 1962, when Finlay showed her the work of the Brazilian Concrete poets published in the anthology *Poesia Concreta*, Mary Ellen Solt was inspired to compose her flower poems, with the collaboration of the typographer John Dearstyne. Works include: *Flowers in Concrete* (University of Indiana Press, 1966); *Concrete Poetry: A World View* (University of Indiana Press, 1970).

THEODORE SPENCER (1902–1949), born in Villanova, Pennsylvania. Spencer was a distinguished scholar of Elizabethan literature at Harvard University, where he was a vital influence on the poets, including Robert Lowell, Delmore Schwartz, and John Berryman, who attended that institution during the late thirties and forties. Works include: *The Paradox in the Circle* (New Directions, 1941).

GERTRUDE STEIN (1874–1946), born in Pennsylvania. The delphic gibberish of Gertrude Stein's writings resists being translated into common sense, but her influence today is as high as it once was in Paris. Works include: *Selected Writings* (Random House, 1962).

JAMES STEPHENS (1882–1950), born in Dublin, Ireland. Along with Joyce and Yeats, Stephens was one of the leaders of the Irish literary renaissance. He is as celebrated today for his *The Crock of Gold* and *Irish Fairy Tales* as for his poems. Works include: *Collected Poems* (Macmillan, 1954).

WALLACE STEVENS (1879–1955), born in Reading, Pennsylvania. He was all of his airs and, for all of his airs, he *was* all of his airs. And we are his heirs. Works include: *The Collected Poems* (Knopf, 1954); *Opus Posthumous: Poems, Plays, Prose* (Knopf, 1957).

MARK STRAND (1934–   ), born in Summerside, Prince Edward Island, Canada. Strand has lectured and read his poetry at numerous college campuses in the United States and Canada. Works include: *Sleeping with One Eye Open* (Atheneum, 1964); *Reasons for Moving* (Atheneum, 1968); *Darker* (Atheneum, 1970).

MAY SWENSON (1919–   ), born in Logan, Utah. The poet has lectured and read widely at colleges throughout the United States. Her play, *The Floor*, was produced at The American Place Theater in 1966. Works include: *A Cage of Spines* (Rinehart, 1958); *To Mix with Time* (Scribner's, 1963); *Half Sun, Half Sleep* (Scribner's, 1967).

SARA TEASDALE (1884–1933), born in St. Louis, Missouri. Miss Teasdale, who died of an overdose of sleeping pills, wrote lyrics as bleakly confessional as any by Sylvia Plath. She is still a strangely haunting presence and witness in this era of Women's Liberation. Works include: *Collected Poems* (Macmillan, 1937).

JAMES TATE (1943–   ), born in Kansas City, Missouri. Tate has read his poetry and lectured at colleges across the country. Works include: *The Lost Pilot* (Yale, 1967); *The Oblivion Ha-Ha* (Atlantic-Little, Brown, 1970).

MELVIN BEAUNORUS TOLSON (1900–1966), born in Moberly, Missouri. Only Book I, "The Curator," of Tolson's epic *Harlem Gallery* was completed before his death. Despite critical acclaim from Theodore Roethke, Robert Frost, and Allen Tate, his achievement as a poet is still largely unrecognized by readers both black and white. Works include: *Rendezvous with America* (Twayne, 1950); *Libretto for the Republic of Liberia* (Twayne, 1953); *Harlem Gallery* (Twayne, 1965).

CHARLES TOMLINSON (1927–   ), born in Stoke-on-Trent, England. Tomlinson has lived and worked many years in the United States, though his poetry is indubitably English in tone and sensibility. Works include: *Seeing Is Believing* (Oxford University Press, 1960); *A Peopled Landscape* (Oxford University Press, 1963); *American Scenes* (Oxford University Press, 1966).

DIANE WAKOSKI (1937–   ), born in Whittier, California. Ms. Wakoski was one of the *Four Young Lady Poets* in a collection edited by LeRoi Jones (Totem Press, 1962). She lives in New York City. Works include: *Inside the Blood Factory* (Doubleday, 1968); *The Motorcycle Betrayal* (Simon & Schuster, 1972).

JOHN HALL WHEELOCK (1886–   ), born on Long Island, New York. A critic and editor as well as a poet, Wheelock has continued to produce work of grace and power until well into his eighties. Works include: *By Daylight and In Dream: New and Collected Poems 1904–1970* (Scribner's, 1970).

JOHN WHEELWRIGHT (1897–1940), born in Boston, Massachusetts. As one of the "pure products of America" that W. C. Williams once wrote about in his famous poem, "To Elsie," the Back Bay blueblood Wheelwright did not "go crazy" but became a poet whose haunted and visionary style has received wide recognition today. He was notorious in Boston during the depression years of the thirties as a political agitator and pamphleteer. Works include: *Political Self-Portrait* (Bruce Humphries, 1940); *Mirrors of Venus* (Bruce Humphries, 1938); *Selected Poems* (New Directions, 1941).

RICHARD WILBUR (1921–   ), born in New York City. Wilbur has translated several of Molière's plays for the stage in recent years. And as a poet, he has received both the Pulitzer Prize and the National Book Award. Works include: *The Poems of Richard Wilbur* (Harcourt Brace & World, 1963).

EMMETT WILLIAMS (1925–   ), born in Greenville, South Carolina. One of the most enterprising and inventive of the Concrete poets, he has been a Johnny Appleseed of the good word in the United States and in Europe. Works include: *An Anecdoted Topography of Chance* (Something Else Press, 1966); *sweethearts* (Something Else Press, 1967); *An Anthology of Concrete Poetry* (Something Else Press, 1967).

JONATHAN WILLIAMS (1929–   ), born in Asheville, North Carolina. Williams has trudged more than six thousand miles on foot through the Appalachians and in Great Britain in search of the authentic speech which is the stuff of poetry, and has lectured widely in universities both here and in Europe. As founder and director of the Jargon Press in 1951, he has published the poems of Mina Loy, as well as collections by outstanding younger poets. Works include: *An Ear in Bartram's Tree* (University of North Carolina Press, 1969); *The Loco Logodaedalist in Situ: Selected Poems 1968–1970* (Cape Goliard Press, 1972).

WILLIAM CARLOS WILLIAMS (1883–1963), born in Rutherford, New Jersey. Williams' unwobbling pivot throughout his life: "No ideas but in things," and his exact sense of the weight and duration of words in his poems have made him one of the most widely admired and imitated poets of his generation. Works include: *The Collected Later Poems* (New Directions, 1950); *The Collected Earlier Poems* (New Directions, 1951); *Pictures from Breughel and Other Poems* (New Directions, 1952); *Paterson, Books I–V* (New Directions, 1963).

YVOR WINTERS (1900–1968), born in Chicago, Illinois. Winters' early poetry was written under the influence of the modernist school of Pound, W. C. Williams, Hart Crane and Marianne Moore, but he began to write in traditional forms, using classical meters and a rationalist syntax, in 1927. His critical essays, collected in *Positivism and Decadence* and *In Defence of Reason*, have been as influential as his poetry. Works include: *Collected Poems* (Swallow Press, 1960).

JAMES WRIGHT (1927–   ), born in Martins Ferry, Ohio. A translator (with Robert Bly) of the poetry of Neruda and Vallejo from the Spanish, Wright currently teaches at Hunter College in New York. He has lectured and read his poetry at various colleges throughout the United States. Works include: *Collected Poems* (Wesleyan University Press, 1971).

PEDRO XISTO (1901–   ), born in Pernambuco, Brazil. Currently serving as cultural attaché of Brazil in Tokyo, Xisto is a diplomat and literary critic as well as a Concrete poet. His poems have appeared in the Brazilian literary review *Invençao* and in anthologies of Concrete poetry throughout the world. Works include: *haikais e concretos (haikus and concrete poems)* (1962).

LOUIS ZUKOVSKY (1904–   ), born in New York City. Zukovsky was one of the prime movers of the Objectivist school in the United States after World War I, but it was not until the sixties that his work came into prominence. With the poet Basil Bunting, he was an early associate of Ezra Pound at Rapallo, Italy. Works include: *All: Collected Short Poems, 1923–1958* (Norton, 1965); *All: Collected Short Poems, 1956–1964* (Norton, 1966); *"A" 1–12* (Doubleday, 1967).

Index of First Lines